MW0061 1428

READER BONUS!

Dear Reader,

As a thank you for your support, Action Takers Publishing would like to offer you a special reader bonus: a free download of our course, How to Write, Publish, Market & Monetize Your Book the Fast, Fun & Easy Way." This comprehensive course is designed to provide you with the tools and knowledge you need to bring your book to life and turn it into a successful venture.

The course typically **retails for $499**, but as a valued reader, you can access it for free. To claim your free download, simply follow this link ActionTakersPublishing.com/ workshops - use the discount code "coursefree" to get a 100% discount and start writing your book today.

If we are still giving away this course by the time you're reading this book, head straight over to your computer and start the course now. It's absolutely free.

READER BONUS!

ActionTakersPublishing.com/workshops
discount code "coursefree"

HOW LOVING YOUR WORK
CHANGES YOUR LIFE

THE
JOY
OF
WORK

Email: lynda@actiontakerspublishing.com

Website: www.actiontakerspublishing.com

ISBN # (paperback) 978-1-956665-34-5

ISBN # (Kindle) 978-1-956665-35-2

Published by Action Takers Publishing™

Dedications

I express my profound appreciation to everyone who has supported me while writing "The Joy of Work." Firstly, I want to thank my beloved husband, Michael, for his unwavering support and belief in me. I also want to acknowledge my dear son, who is no longer with us, for watching over me with pride and love. My gratitude also extends to my parents, siblings, and family for always being there for me. I am grateful to Action Takers Publishing and my fellow authors for their patience and hard work in bringing this project to the public. I dedicate this book to all those who have ever worked in jobs they did not enjoy and aspired to do work they love. Your stories have inspired me to write, and I hope our words bring you joy and encouragement on your journey toward finding joy-filled work. Last, but not least, thank you, God, for ideas, words, and the ability to communicate them.

~Whitnie Wiley

To all the colleagues, mentors and friends who have enriched my work and life through our connection.

~Jennifer Persike

I dedicate this chapter to all those who strive to find joy in their work. To those who believe that work is more than a means of survival, it is also an opportunity for growth, fulfillment, and making a positive impact. Let this chapter serve as a reminder that despite challenges, we can find joy in our work. May our dedication to cultivating joy in our work inspire others with our desire to find meaning, purpose, and satisfaction in our daily endeavors.

~Anette Smith

My chapter is dedicated to my daughter Amadi, the brightest light of my life, who reminded me that life is for living and not just for working! And to my dear, departed father, my absolute hero, who taught me that having ideas without action is being on a path that leads nowhere.

~Chineme Noke

To those whose voices remind us of our worth giving us the courage to dream.

~Diane Davidson

I dedicate this chapter to my husband and two children to be blessed beyond measure to find joy in everything that they do and in who they are in their lives!

~Jen M. Clarke

To the women who have lifted me up time and time again. I promise to pay it forward.

~Katie Evans

This chapter is dedicated to my children, Kristofer Williams and Gabrielle Outsey. They are my why. I hope that because they see me creating the life of my dreams, they know and attain the life of theirs.

~Keri White

I dedicate these heartfelt thoughts to the educators across the world who are the quiet heroes that go unseen and rarely heard. To these leaders of the next generations who are sacrificing their lives to serve and protect the vulnerable within our school walls, I humbly express my prayers of gratitude. I dedicate these words to you for your service to the most valued piece of society, our children.

~Khalil Sikander

To all the amazing people in my true network.

~Leah Hoyer

To my family and friends who have stood by my side throughout this roller coaster ride.

~Nicole Townsend

I cannot imagine a more fitting person to dedicate this chapter to than my best friend Wendy Story-Cordon who came into my life thirty-four years ago through work and my life was forever changed. You have been a non-stop champion of supporting my purpose, one of the most essential PEOPLE in my life and no question the one I have the most PLAYFUL moments in life with. While our life paths have taken us on many journeys, we make EFFORT every day to cultivate our friendship and stay close. Wendy, it is from our friendship from work put to practice in our lives that has made this chapter possible, with love Pam.

~Pam Marcheski

This chapter is dedicated to my partner, Stephanie. I'm often surprised by what I can accomplish just by knowing that you've got my back. Also, I would be remiss if I didn't mention my good friends, Debbie DeVries, and Whitnie Wiley. Your support literally made this possible.

~Robert Hilliard

I dedicate this chapter to Whitnie Wiley for your friendship, support, advice and encouragement. To my son Logan, my sister Marsha and my dear friend Jackie (who I miss with all my heart) - I thank God and my angels every day for each of you and am so blessed to have you grace my life. And to all the action takers out there who are taking action to read this book and make your dreams come true - I believe in you!

~Shelly Buettner

This chapter is dedicated to my Dad, James Mays Sr. He was a hard-working man that made sure his family was well taken care of. Without his labor and love for his family, I would not be the person I am today. He is in heaven, and I know he is watching and saying, Great Job!

~Sheryl Mays

To my grandmas Masha and Vera, on the other side of this mortal veil. Your work ethics, your undeniable zeal for life, and your passion for your families and causes lives on through me. I love you. I miss you. And I celebrate your lives daily through joy in my work.

~Victoria Rader, Ph.D.

Table of Contents

Introduction

Welcome to a revolution in the way you perceive work—welcome to "The Joy of Work: How Loving Your Work Changes Your Life."

Do you find yourself among the multitudes who dread the morning alarm, burdened by the realization that another day of uninspiring work awaits? Are your precious hours being consumed in the pursuit of someone else's vision? Does the word 'work' evoke a sense of drudgery rather than delight?

Now, imagine a world where you are driven by passion, where each task is an opportunity for growth, and where you wake up each morning inspired by your profession. Envision a life where your work aligns with your dreams, kindling joy not just in you but creating ripples of positivity around you.

"The Joy of Work: How Loving Your Work Changes Your Life" is more than just a book—it's a guide to transforming your existence. Inside these pages, you will discover the journeys of 20 extraordinary individuals. From committed employees to audacious entrepreneurs, these are people who have taken the reins of their professional lives and forged their paths. They are the ones who have discovered not just the joy in their work but also found the secret to winning at life—every single day.

Remember, the way we expend our days is, in essence, the way we spend our lives. If you're ensnared in a job that you despise, it's likely that your life may feel devoid of joy and fulfillment. Isn't it time you pivoted towards a life where work becomes a source of inspiration and achievement? Where you can embrace your profession with love, thereby unlocking the door to a life brimming with purpose and dreams realized?

Join us as we redefine what it means to work and live. Discover the secret to transforming your professional life into a beacon of joy and success in "The Joy of Work." Embark on this journey and take the first step towards the life of your dreams.

CHAPTER 1

Joy Is an Inside Game

by Whitnie Wiley

You're the reason your career sucks! That was harsh, but it's true. One of the failings of many workers, particularly American workers, is the thought that our jobs should make us happy.

Au contraire, mon frère! You are supposed to take your contentedness and your happiness to your job. And, if your job makes you happy—that's gravy.

Don't get me wrong, I know some jobs blow, and the manager you work for is the worst. I've been there. But I've discovered on my journey that all the time and energy I spent waiting for things to get better was wasted and better spent being happy—then taking action.

Whatever happened at work, I was responsible for placing myself in environments aligned with and expending energy to convert those environments into places I wanted to work. Therefore, my happiness, in and away from work, depends on me.

I had some work experiences that I enjoyed immensely, that barely paid enough to get my car off the parking lot after the shift, and others, despite being paid a king's ransom, where I was miserable. I've learned over my four-plus decades of work that happiness is an inside job. Even when the work is not that great, there are ways to make it enjoyable and, dare say, lovable until something else comes along. If you can't, then you need to change jobs sooner than later.

I will not name any employers or bosses herein to protect the guilty. Still, my work experiences ran the gamut from retail to culinary, entertainment to government, and all kinds of gigs in between, including a failed attempt at entrepreneurship—the last time around, not this one.

The factors that help us enjoy our work differ from what makes us unhappy. You cannot depend on or wait for that to happen. Your career is your business; you must control it to get what you want and need.

The following are three ways you can turn an unsatisfying job situation into something you can grin and bear until you can move on, or if you determine to do so, be happy where you are.

Empower yourself.

The most important thing you can do to turn your job situation around is to take responsibility for where you are and how you feel. You must ask yourself what you are doing to contribute to the problem. When you look around and see incompetence, cruelty, and the like, you're probably thinking, how can any of this be my fault or responsibility?

First, in the energetic sense, you attract the same energy you put out. While you may not have directly created your situation, you control your reaction or response to it. By accepting 100 percent responsibility, you take back control.

Do you feel better about yourself when you control the situation or are at someone else's mercy? Your job is no different. Once you decide to exercise control over your job, you will feel different about your job.

Second, you choose to be in that job daily, even if you think you are there because you're stuck. While, for many reasons, it might not be an easy fix to leave your job, it is your choice that you are there. Similarly, you can choose to go—with or without having developed a plan.

All work is honorable. It doesn't matter if it's dirty or any other adjective; you can find something positive to be grateful for. Some of the bright spots were skills acquired and lessons learned.

Identify and focus on what is good.

Something brought you there—pay, people, perks. This may be hard to accept, but there is something good in every situation. I remember when I was going through my work challenges, all I could see was what was wrong. The more I focused on that, the more there was to see. At one point, I started closing my office door the moment I arrived and only opened it when I needed to leave. A conversation with my coach reminded me I was letting other people and my perceptions about the job keep me unhappy.

I wanted something different. Everything was okay with the job, the people, etc. To get something different, I needed to change. Once accepted, I began developing a strategy and plan to transition to my desired work. Creating a role aligned with my desired skills, abilities, and talents was included.

Hope and light at the end of the tunnel.

Have you noticed you focus on the dark when things seem darkest? You must focus on something else. You got this job; you'll get another. ~Tony Robbins

---

Often, we feel hopeless in a situation and as if things will always be what they are, but change is constant. You have to remember that there was a time when you didn't have this job. There will be a time when you won't have this job.

What do you want? Start to bring the future into the present. Feel it. Live it daily. Watch your attitude change, and then your opportunities open up.

Work, your career, is more than where you go each day or what you do to earn a paycheck. Work has purpose and meaning, even if you don't feel your work is meaningful. Your work can define you or not.

I spent 20 years working in government relations, a portion of which was as a lawyer and a lobbyist. That work had tremendous meaning and importance to the people of the State of California. However, at some point, the work became meaningless for me. For many of the people I worked with, being a lawyer or lobbyist is who they were. It was the culmination of their lifelong dreams and the gateway to everything they wanted, personally and professionally.

For me, it was a job. My job was simply the thing I did. I wanted more.

I wanted my work to mean something to the people I was interacting with, but more importantly, I wanted to find purpose in how I spent my days. Taking control of my career meant figuring out my purpose beyond simply keeping a roof over my head.

My first step was to start to dream. I dreamed about the life I wanted and how work fits into it rather than how I would fit my life around my work.

Your life and career can be anything you want them to be, whether traveling the globe, teaching children, inventing new ideas or products, etc. How you earn your living is up to you, and it's not your parents' dreams, limited to your degrees or what you've been doing.

Studies say the average person will have 11 careers in their lifetime, almost double what it was a short 20 years ago. Continuously evaluate whether what you are doing is aligned with your values and your vision for your life.

My vision is to have a second home in Hawaii, so that I can spend time there, not only on vacations. That means not being tied to a desk job or working for people who require me to show up to a particular location. I aim to work on whatever, wherever, and whenever I want.

What is the vision you have for your work?

The best way to incorporate dreaming into your life is by regularly contemplating what you want and creating an action plan to make it happen.

- Start at the beginning.

- Sit and dream.

- Pen and paper in hand.

- No limitations.

- No impossibilities.

- All possibilities and potentialities.

- Just dream.

Think of all the things you want to do. This exercise is about something other than work or money; it is about getting in touch with what you want to do that excites you to get up each day.

Once you have a clear picture of what you want your life to look and feel like, spend some time delving into why. Once you are clear on those, you can think about how to make it happen and how work fits into the picture.

Annually, or more frequently if you choose, clear a block of time on your calendar and simply sit with pen and paper. You'll want to use pen and paper, rather than your cell phone or other electronic devices for scientific reasons and to minimize distractions.

Play soft and relaxing music to set a mood, then ask yourself, "What do I want?" Then keep asking.

Part of that process will also be to ask why. Studies have shown that it is not enough to know what you want; you also need to understand why. Having a why helps you to be consistent and persistent when obstacles appear and the going gets tough.

I had no reason beyond needing the money for much of my work life or various jobs. There were times when that was all I could muster. Except, it wasn't sustainable when things were so-so.

After getting clarity on the life you want, you can begin addressing how you will financially support that lifestyle. Start by asking, "How can I make money with what's on this list?"

Feel free to modify the questions by asking what kind of work you would do if you could do anything you wanted, without regard for money, time, or any other constraint. Ask those questions, and whatever others come up as many times as possible, in the time you've set aside, until you have no more answers.

You can do soul-singing work by finding ways to turn what's on your list into income-producing activities or use the things on your list as your why for your work, until you can transition to doing what you desire. The good news is with either approach, you have begun taking control of your career and why you are doing it.

You only have one life—one opportunity to live the life of your dreams. That doesn't mean every moment is rainbows and unicorns. However, life is too short to leave your dreams languishing on the vine.

Sometimes you work in careers you don't enjoy, or in a job you love, you'll have tasks and responsibilities you don't like. You may need a job just to have the income to keep a roof over your head or while you work toward a bigger plan. That differs from settling, because it's easier to do than invest the time and energy to transition to what you desire.

Doing work you love and taking control of your career requires courage. It requires taking a chance on the unknown, such as leaving a job to start a business or switching to a new industry or employer.

For years I hated my job. While I didn't ignore what I felt initially, I didn't explore the reason behind it. After accepting I was unhappy, I searched for why. After all, I had a good job, making good money. After much prayer and introspection, I realized it wasn't the work itself. It simply didn't align with my values and priorities.

I was unmotivated in the office and irritable with my family when I returned home at night. My spirit was sucked out of me. I needed to change. And I did. I put together an extrication plan, developed a framework for my next chapter, and created a timeline for the transition.

Now, I wake up every morning joyful. I'm excited and grateful that I get to do what I do for a living. My work matters to my clients and me. I get to do work that taps into my skills, abilities, talents, and creativity, and I take great delight in making an immediate difference in other people's lives.

So, how did I get here?

I wish it were as easy as dreaming a dream, snapping my fingers, and it comes true. Nothing could be further from the truth. My journey was filled with doubt, fear, and self-loathing.

My earliest memory of what I wanted to be when I grew up was to be a lawyer. After discovering that one of my cousins wanted to be a lawyer, I switched to wanting to be a doctor—more specifically, a pediatrician. I'm unsure why either was on my radar, as no one I knew was a doctor or lawyer. Those are not professions I remember talking with my parents about.

The path to my career as a doctor was cut short, in my sophomore year of college, when I failed to pass organic chemistry. It got worse from there. After graduating from high school a year ahead of schedule and getting an early start to college; I managed, in two years, to meet a guy, fall in love, transfer schools to be closer to him, and drop out of school, because I was not mature enough to be away from home. After that fiasco, I worked for a year before returning home to start over at a community college and transferring to a different university.

When I started at the University of California, Berkeley, I thought I was academically back on track. However, I had yet to create a life or work plan. That lack of focus and, more importantly, why I was doing what I was doing, ended up costing me more time, resulting in my flunking out of college and being academically dismissed.

That greatly impacted my self-esteem and how I proceeded in the future. Where I had been relatively fearless in my decision-making up until then, the academic obstacles and poor life choices left me battered and bruised. I found it harder to take chances, especially since, by that point, I'd gotten married, had a child, divorced, and had to provide financially for myself and my son.

My Berkeley experience was a blip, a detour on the road to where I am. Despite not graduating, I eventually went to law school, a story for another time, and started my career as a lawyer and lobbyist. After deciding to go in a different direction, I returned to get my undergraduate and graduate degrees in another area.

While I don't kick myself for my path and choices, and all my experiences have served a purpose, bringing me to where I am today, I also recognize that the lessons I learned on my journey can benefit someone else. As hard as it may seem to believe, my joy is derived from the fact that my experiences are not wasted. They are not wasted.

Ask yourself why, if you find yourself in a job or career you don't love. Figure out what you are getting out of the situation and whether there is a better way. Maybe you will stay, but make a plan to leave. Or, in the short term, you get another position or hobby that allows you to do what you love, to express the positive and creative aspects of your being.

Whichever you choose, you're in control. Whether you think you are or not, you're in control. Every action is a choice of commission or omission. You might also choose what works for you and allows you to take control of your career.

When you choose to be in control of your work and your feelings surrounding it, joy flows.

Whitnie Wiley

Whitnie Wiley is a strategist specializing in organizational, leadership, and employee development. Having experienced poor work cultures and inadequate leadership in various companies, Whitnie now focuses on assisting organizations and individuals in adopting effective strategies that foster positive workplaces and cultures.

As a highly sought-after coach, speaker, and trainer, Whitnie shares valuable insights from her personal and client experiences with a blend of grace, humility, and humor. Her aim is to drive positive change in today's business landscape.

Connect with Whitnie at https://www.linkedin.com/in/whitniewiley.

CHAPTER 2

Be Happy Now

by Dr. Janice Doucet Thompson

Dedication: Deep gratitude to Dr. Marshall Goldsmith for inspiring and motivating me, and thousands of others, to Be Happy Now.

Be Happy Now ~ life is too short.

If the past few years have taught me anything, it is that life is precious and our time on this Earth may be shorter than we expect. It's not unusual to feel sad or helpless as you navigate the changes in your life. Like me, you might be grieving for family or friends who are no longer here, feel the loss of connection to others because of differing beliefs, or miss those who still don't feel safe enough to reengage in the world. Adopting a mindset of happiness has helped me manage these challenges, persevere with positivity, and change my life for the better.

According to scientific research, happiness is an emotional state characterized by feelings of joy, satisfaction, contentment, and fulfillment. While happiness has many different definitions, it involves positive emotions and life satisfaction. It is not something you can turn on and off as you begin and end your day and it's unreasonable to think you can be happy all of the time. However, embracing happiness may be a positive emotion that sparks joy in your life and helps you live longer.

Dr. Sonja Lyubomirsky, a psychology professor at University of California Riverside, maintains we all have a happiness *set point*. When extremely positive or negative events happen—such as buying your first house or losing a job—they temporarily increase or decrease our happiness, but we eventually drift back to our set point. Interestingly, Dr. Lyubomirsky and others have found that our genetic set point is responsible for only about fifty percent of our happiness, life circumstances affect about ten percent, and a whopping forty percent is completely up to us. That means a substantial portion of your happiness, under your control, is determined by your habits, attitude, and outlook on life.

I have always been an optimist and chose optimism as my word of the year for 2021 after living in isolation for a year due to the pandemic. Why? I believe that without hope we lose touch with the emotion that allows optimism and happiness, to evolve in ourselves. Psychologists have identified two types of happiness: *experienced* happiness and *remembered* happiness. We tend to remember and ruminate on high points and low points in our life. Indeed, experiencing happiness is the sum of the little joys throughout the day.

Work has always played a meaningful role for happiness in my life. Although I can't document it, I'm quite certain that at age twelve, I was the first newspaper girl in Waltham, Massachusetts. It was the late

1960s and I inherited the paper route from my older brother. I still re-member the joy I got from my first job delivering the Boston Globe and the Press Tribune and the tips I earned from my satisfied customers. I also worked part-time jobs throughout high school, because my parents set the example of hard work. It allowed me to buy things I wanted on my own and feel independent. This prepared me for, when I was enter-ing my senior year of high school and my parents relocated to southern California, my being allowed to stay behind and complete the year in Massachusetts.

College took me to the West Coast. I got a job in public affairs when I graduated from San Jose State University. Several careers and corpo-rate jobs later (in communications, public relations, sales, marketing, training and development) brought me to where I am today. In 2009, after thirty years of working for others, I realized that I needed to be my own boss, launch my consulting practice, and own my happiness. It took a toxic workplace to impact me in some very unhealthy ways to finally come to this decision. I hadn't been considering the long hours I was working and the drain it was having on me personally and pro-fessionally. Alcohol became my coping mechanism, pouring a glass (or two) of wine each night after a tough day, which was every day. I real-ized I wasn't living a fulfilled life. Instead, my energy went to pleasing an unreasonable bully boss. I remember asking her, "What do you want from me, just tell me and I'll do it." I replayed that scene a hundred times before I said, "enough!"

Now, I tell people I never want to retire, I love what I do so much that I could easily do it forever. Master Coach Marshall Goldsmith writes in *The Earned Life* that the luckiest people on earth are the ones who can say, "I get paid to do for a living what I would gladly do for free." I wholeheartedly agree. My work brings me so much joy and satisfaction when I help others be the best version of themselves. As an executive coach, my practice is focused on C-suite leaders and business owners who are already very successful, but need to focus on changing one or two habits that are holding them back from being more effective leaders.

My *why* or purpose as an executive coach is to help organizations, teams and individuals realize their potential. To be their best in order to achieve success. I believe you have to love what you do in life (too many people don't!) to find true success. For me, that means working hard at work that I love. I believe that in order to lead and inspire others you have to create an emotional connection with them. As Howard Gardner's research showed, people are able to effect real change only when their emotions are engaged.

My mom inspired me to be a life-long learner. She returned to school in her early fifties to attend Ventura Community College and earned an associate degree. She was a significant role model and still is at eighty-nine years old. Learning agility is one of my personal values, because I believe it promotes diversity of thought, continuous growth, and personal development. I am the first person in my immediate and extended family to earn a bachelor's, master's, and a doctorate degree. I continue to grow and learn something new every day.

That said, there is nothing wrong with retirement. It's what co-authors Ken Blanchard and Morton Shaevitz believe and what they write about in *Refire Don't Retire.* It is the time of your life to refire as an antidote to retirement (I give this book to all my retiring clients). The idea is embracing the years ahead with enthusiasm (happiness) rather than apathy. They ask, "What are you going to do with the rest of your life to make it healthy, joyful, and meaningful?"

Have you ever told yourself: "I'll be happy when _____ (fill in the blank)."

Here are some responses that I've said quietly to myself… "I'll be happy when I get that promotion…when I lose fifteen pounds…when I launch my business and quit my job"… and on, and on, and on.

I remember thinking at one corporate job, "I'll be happy when I get my earned place at the executive table." Sadly, when I finally got there, I was shocked and disappointed to discover that it wasn't for me. I couldn't relate to the manly speak and I didn't even like the executives around the table.

All those years working so hard to get somewhere better and I wasn't happy when I got there. Sound familiar? I learned that one idea behind **Be Happy Now** is bringing mindfulness in to improve my performance. My great friend and mindfulness coach Pam Marcheski helped me learn to be open, non-judgmental, particularly of myself, and in the moment. She taught me the tools to relax my mind, focus, and change my mindset. It is something I practice every day.

I've learned it's about living your best life now and maintaining an optimistic view of the future. We all sometimes ruminate about a mistake we made, a missed opportunity, or some other negative experience. Author Sally Helgesen writes in *How Women Rise* that it's a habit that does not serve women (or men) well. She's right.

It is much better to flip the conversation in your head to focus on today and tomorrow. Life is too short to ruminate on our past mistakes. We need to make peace with our past, learn from it, and resolve to solve our problems today so we can move on with our lives and a better future.

If you want to achieve joy at work and *Be Happy Now,* find ways to practice being **H-A-P-P-Y**. I call them HAPPY habits that you can practice throughout the day.

Harness positive energy. Avoid people with negative energy. They suck the happiness out of a room like a Dyson® vacuum beats your rug. One colleague exemplified this idea in every way. She was an advocate of catching people doing things right, not focusing on what went wrong. That helped her and her team be more successful and happier. So choose wisely and embrace positive people. Research shows you'll live longer if you are more optimistic and positive in nature.

Acknowledge your mistakes, and then move on. My great friend Garry Ridge, former CEO of WD-40®, believes you don't make mistakes, you have learning moments. In his company, employees (known as tribe members) learn from mistakes, forgive, and let go, and tell themselves they'll do better next time. Garry and his team created a world class culture at WD-40® by implementing this idea. We all need to learn, adapt and thrive in ambiguous or new situations. Our ability to continuously have learning moments will determine the extent to which you thrive and find joy in work.

Plan to make peace with your past. It's easy to say, but hard to do. Research shows women are more forgiving of others than men are. This is due to personality traits such as agreeableness, empathy, and the value women place on relationships. Being able to forgive ourselves is especially difficult for women, but necessary, nonetheless. I remember feeling powerless when I realized I couldn't change the culture at one company and my staff was suffering, but I had to let go and I hope that was an example to others that sometimes you just have to move on.

Power up your joy. It's never too late to accelerate your joy meter. One powerful, long-lasting habit is doing one thing each day that brings you joy. That's 1,140 minutes of joyful opportunities. Focus on one and more will come. Research shows we work harder when we are happier at work.

You go first! At the end of my life, I want to say, "I lived happy, and I brought fulfillment and joy to others." My word for 2023 is fulfillment – a word that means happiness and satisfaction. Remember, you go first. As an executive coach, I've learned that the most successful leaders I work with do this intuitively. They aren't ashamed to ask for help. It's one reason that they are so successful.

I've also learned that life is too short to wait for your happiness. You have the power to bring happiness into your life now. It might be the only thing you truly control. If you can't find the courage to let it go, you'll have a challenging time living a happy life. Letting it go is a good habit to practice if you tend to live in the past and are always looking for something or someone else to make you happy.

In the end, it is important to forgive yourself for your past mistakes and strive to **Be Happy Now**. Here are some tips to try:

- Start by finding something new to do every day. One thing that will bring happiness to you and the people around you. If you choose to live a happy life, you will be surprised at how it will impact your attitude and your success.

- Find an accountability partner. My dear friend and author Pat Zigarmi and I have a ritual. We talk on the phone every other week for fifteen minutes about our goals and what makes us happy, or not. We call it *Doing Life Together* (inspired by Sally Helgesen). It helps us keep an eye on what's most important and hold one another accountable for our goals and dreams.

- Ask for help when you need it. When I launched my consulting practice over a decade ago, after a successful thirty years in corporate life, I was uncertain that I could make it work. I obsessed with all the details of running a business and forgot to lean into the good people who supported me in the first place.

My coaching practice has taught me that successful people know when and how to ask for help. Now, I'm not afraid to ask for help and I'm constantly amazed with and grateful for those people who will go out of their way to help me.

Another practice that helped me was redefining my personal values. In my quest to become a credible consultant, I had to fully comprehend the values, beliefs, ethics and ideals that drive me. This was a huge lesson – in order to do what you say, you first have to understand what you *want* to say. This exercise helped me define and prioritize my top five values: Relationships, Integrity, Learning, Health, and Happiness. The first three were values that helped me succeed in my corporate career: creating an emotional connection with others through strong relationships, building credibility by keeping promises, and thriving as a life-long learner. Like completing my doctorate in organizational leadership at age fifty-nine.

The last two values – Health and Happiness – were the result of moving into my new role as a business owner and consultant. Leaving that last job improved my health as I left the toxic environment and all the stink that was associated with it. Health and happiness became the result of finding a new focus to **Be Happy Now** and pursue the work I love.

The Dalai Lama believes the purpose of our lives is to be happy. He writes, "Human happiness and human satisfaction most ultimately come from within oneself." I hope my story will be your invitation to more joy and, ultimately, more happiness. Remember, focus on living one joyful moment each day and more will come.

Dr. Janice Doucet Thompson

Dr. Janice Doucet Thompson is founder and managing principal of JD Thompson & Associates based in Sacramento, CA. Dr. Thompson launched her consulting practice in 2009 on her quest to step out of the corporate rat race and live a more happy, fulfilling and joyful life.

She is best known as a Leadership Coach to C-Suite Executives. Dr. Thompson helps emerging and established executives step into top-level leadership roles with "all in" confidence. She is a certified Marshall Goldsmith Stakeholder Centered Coach and has coached hundreds of executives and their teams to be even more successful.

With more than thirty years of experience as an internal/external consultant in a diverse group of industries, Dr. Thompson understands what it takes to deliver results in challenging and complex environments. She has identified her top five personal values as Relationships, Integrity, Learning, Health and Happiness. While they are all important, her values build on one another. Dr. Thompson believes that living each value helps her Be Happy Now to win at the work she loves.

Her purpose is…To help people be their best so they can live more productive, happier and joyful lives.

Connect with Janice at

https://www.linkedin.com/in/drjanicedoucetthompson.

CHAPTER 3

Let's Connect!
How Making Connections
Changes Everything

by Jennifer Persike

We humans need connection.

Never was this more evident than during the pandemic. Connection became currency as we navigated life in isolation away from family, friends, co-workers, and classmates.

According to the World Happiness Report published in March 2021, "the reduction in the physical availability of social connections [during the pandemic] is concerning, as over a century of research has proven how crucial social connection is for well-being."

This was certainly true for me. In isolation, I looked for every opportunity to create connection, and I was not alone!

We found all types of ways to stay connected. Zoom and other platforms provided the vehicle for happy hours, book clubs, yoga, high school reunions, and so much more. Remember the car parades to celebrate birthdays and graduations?

After adjusting to life at home, sanitizing mail and doing my own hair, I shifted to how I could stay connected professionally.

I started a new group via Zoom to pull together young professionals in my industry, helped create on-line events, and joined a virtual meditation group.

Why did we do these things?

Bestselling author and researcher Dr. Brene' Brown tells us, "Connection is the energy that exists between people when they feel seen, heard, and valued; when they can give and receive without judgment; and when they derive sustenance and strength from the relationship."

We know that many of us seek connection in our personal lives, but what about our work life? What role does connection play in our job satisfaction and success? Why do we need to place a priority on making connections?

It should come as no surprise to learn that those with connections at work perform better in their job, and are happier and healthier. According to the 2017 State of the American Workplace Report by Gallup, Inc., 70% of employees report "connection to colleagues is a crucial element of a happy work life." Further, the reports states, "employees who have strong relationships at work are more engaged, produce a better work product, and are more physically and emotionally healthy."

Connections at work are critical to success in your professional life. They certainly have been in mine.

I spent more than three decades leading associations and non-profit organizations and working in the public affairs arena, where making contacts was part of the job. I came to understand, however, that moving beyond initial contacts to create valued connections is both personally rewarding and pays off professionally.

My first introduction to the importance of connections came from my own father. He was a dentist at a time when it was frowned upon to advertise. Instead, he joined Rotary and the California Dental Association to make connections that could lead to new patients as well as long-lasting friendships.

Looking back on each chapter of my 30-plus year career, connections have been a key ingredient every step of the way. During my last semester at Chico State, my favorite professor introduced me to two former students who had already launched their careers. That introduction led me to become a member of a professional public relations organization, a move to a new city upon graduation, and helped me secure my first entry level career role at a small-town chamber of commerce.

The importance of connections grew from there, leading to almost every other career opportunity. From a paid internship immediately after my college graduation, to a publication's role for an agricultural organization, to a public information officer position at a regional electric utility, and — finally — the big jump to a management position with a statewide association. In each case, my connections led to a recommendation or a great job opportunity and to the building of a successful career.

Finally, in 2018, I left my position with the association to launch my own firm, Jennifer Persike & Company. Once again, I tapped into my connections for help on everything from finding a good accountant, to marketing and preparing proposals. As a one-person firm, I didn't have the "built in" team that I had become accustomed to during my career. To stay connected with peers and other professionals, I took on-line courses, attended conferences and networking events, and volunteered to speak on panels.

Through all the roles I played, I came to understand that the connections I cultivated both inside and outside the various organizations created a sense of fulfillment and job satisfaction. They helped me to grow professionally and climb the ladder to positions of leadership.

The Scientific American reports that, "connection on the job is the ingredient that motivates us and creates a sense of deeper satisfaction." Because we spend one-third of our lives working, most of us are looking for a sense of fulfillment in addition to a paycheck. Whether we know it or not, we are looking for "connection."

As a leader, I found that connecting with my team and helping them to connect with each other was essential to creating workplace cultures where my team thrived and collaborated to make big things happen. This connection fostered a sense of teamwork and shared vision and resulted in a "well-oiled" machine that executed at a high level. It also helped me and my staff build valuable relationships…even friendships that have endured long after the job.

Think about it…look behind every successful leader and you'll see an army of connections. I found that taking the time to connect with those I lead – "getting to know them as people" is a strategic discipline that reaps numerous benefits.

Improving genuine rapport helps to build trust and gain insights and perspectives about what your folks are doing and what they think of the organization. You understand how to better support them and how they can support you.

I developed a simple way over the years to cultivate connections with my team.

1) **Ask Questions**: Put your reporter hat on and take a genuine interest. Ask questions and listen more than you talk. According to Marshall Goldsmith, renowned executive coach, author and international speaker, listening is the most important skill of a successful leader.

2) **Find Common Ground**: As you interact, you will likely discover shared experiences or interests. These points of connection can help to open new pathways of discovery and communication.

3) **Gain Valuable Insights**: When we connect with our team members, we gain new perspectives and information. New ways of looking at old problems can lead to breakthroughs and problem solving. You also can discover how to tap into the talents of your staff and how to best empower and develop them.

4) **Connect with Your Team**: Beyond the one-on-one connection, I invested time and energy in helping to build my team by creating opportunities to connect with each other. We would take time to celebrate milestones such as weddings, babies, landmark birthdays and more.

Beyond my own team, I learned that creating connections up and down the organization was equally important. Let's face it, we can't succeed in an organization unless we have support from others. Once I was promoted to an executive level role in my organization, I found myself shifting from what had been a "peer-to-peer" relationship with those who had been my co-managers to a "boss-to-peer" relationship.

This can be difficult. I knew that continuing to connect with those with whom I had relationships, and in other cases building new connection with staff I did not know well, was essential. Once again, I used the intentional path described above to show interest and build true connection. It took time, but we got there. I demonstrated visible support and the favor was returned.

Meaningful connection is a two-way street. Both parties can gain from the relationship. We benefit by sharing common interests, values, and challenges on the job or personally. The adage, "if you scratch my back, I'll scratch yours," comes to mind.

I placed a high value on connection with my co-workers. But I also knew that continued professional growth required me to increase connections outside my organization. Beyond the nine to five, I joined professional groups, attended events, and collected a lot of business cards.

How many times have you attended a conference and come home with a briefcase full of business cards that you ignore? How often have you accepted or made an invitation on social media and let it languish? How many of us are meeting dozens of new people through virtual meetings that do not go beyond the screen?

It isn't just a numbers game — building true connections takes intention and investment. Sitting alone in your in-person or virtual office will not get you there.

As I continued to make connections and broaden my network, other opportunities emerged. Seeking connections with folks who were in other industries, from different backgrounds...who had different life experiences gave my life greater meaning and a true sense of joy.

Most of us at some point may start to feel stuck in a job, an organization, or a specific industry.

Broadening our connections can open a new world of possibilities. Connections led to my involvement in local, statewide, and national issues and organizations. I was invited to serve on non-profit boards of directors, I volunteered to lead initiatives, and organized and spoke at conferences around the world.

This connectivity and visibility allowed me to take the leap to start my own company. Like my father, connections led to new clients and collaborations with other entrepreneurs.

At every stage of my career, I built meaningful connections with amazing people and they in turn have connected with me. You can do this, too. Your connections will create a community of allies that will give your work added meaning and help you succeed. Like mine, these connections may also become valued relationships, even friendships that you will cherish for years to come.

Here are some steps to get you connecting outside your organization:

Begin by identifying individuals with whom you currently work inside and outside of your organization. Who inspires you? Who did you meet at a conference that you would like to know better? Who can give you advice? Who can help expand your knowledge of a different industry or role? Who could mentor you or make an introduction? You get the idea. Think about how connections can help you grow professionally.

After you have identified people in your world with whom you would like to connect, develop a plan to make it happen. Start with a specific goal, such as, "I want to increase my knowledge of what it takes to serve on a non-profit board of directors." Next, identify connections you might know who currently serve on boards. If you do not have a direct contact that can help you, who in your trusted network can you tap to make an introduction? Finding avenues to build greater connection can take many forms.

Get involved with a trade association, serve on a board of directors or committee with a professional organization, or volunteer to support a non-profit in your community. Whatever path you choose, these endeavors are rewarding and take you out of the everyday work routine. Seeking broader connection provides professional growth opportunities outside of your current role.

Once you have made an initial contact, how do you turn that into a meaningful connection? Try these strategies to get you started.

- Schedule time weekly to make and build connections

- Be open and authentic in your interaction

- Get to know a person's story and share your own

- Find common ground and interests

- Check-in regularly with your connections

- Ask for support and be supportive

- Help others make connections!

Over time you will find that meaningful connections become allies and trusted advisors who you can tap along your career path. It worked for me...it changed my life, and it can change yours, too!

Jennifer Persike

Jennifer Persike is an innovative strategist and a visionary leader with more than 30 years of experience leading and working with California water and energy utilities, statewide associations, non-profits, and corporations.

In 2017, Jennifer established Jennifer Persike & Company. She and her team help organizations and individuals to lead better and do better. JP & Co. specializes in consultation for critical business needs, including organizational optimization, strategic planning, leadership development and training, and external affairs. The firm also is committed to helping clients organically integrate diversity, inclusion, and equity into their company values.

Ms. Persike is past Executive Director of Leadership California, a statewide non-profit dedicated to increasing the representation and influence of diverse women leaders in all sectors across California.

As former Deputy Executive Director for the Association of California Water Agencies (ACWA), Ms. Persike built a reputation for understanding the issues, people, and challenges in the water arena. She drove numerous high-profile, successful external and internal initiatives and oversaw operations and external affairs.

Ms. Persike is committed to giving back to the community, serving on numerous boards including the American Red Cross-Gold Country Region, ACWA Foundation, Water Education Foundation, Association for Women in Water, Energy and the Environment, and Alzheimer's Association.

Ms. Persike holds a bachelor's degree in Journalism and Political Science from Chico State University. She holds a Certification in Facilitation, Mediation and Arbitration from University of California, Davis; a Marshall Goldsmith Stakeholder Centered Coaching Certification; and is completing her certificate in DE&I through Cornell University.

Connect with Jennifer at www.linkedin.com/in/jenniferpersike.

CHAPTER 4

---•❀•---

The Power of Meaningful Work: Finding Joy and Fulfillment

by Anette Smith

555. This number resonates in my head often. Why? It is the number of California registered nurses that graduated from a public/private collaborative program. A program I created for the health system I previously worked for. For the purpose of this book, let's call them the Health System. At the time of the project's creation, the region where I lived had a shortage of 1,000 nurses. That shortage would only worsen as we anticipated a silver tsunami of retirements. In collaboration with three other health systems, they funded the expansion of a local nursing program with slots specifically for current employees that had trouble getting into a nursing program. The challenge the participants had was one of space limitations, and not ability.

However, Health System X wanted to do even more. They had an excellent fiscal year and, as an anchor nonprofit organization, committed to supporting the communities in which they practiced. They wanted to give back to our communities in a meaningful way. We were told there were too many variables that would impede our progress:

- Lack of nursing faculty

- Lack of clinical faculty

- Lack of classroom space

- Lack of clinical laboratory space

- Lack of available clinical rotations

Frankly, it couldn't be done. Way too many barriers. Impossible. Never been done before. There is a benefit to being ignorant of the impossible. Somehow, my colleagues and I were able to address each and every one of those challenges. It wasn't easy, and mistakes were made! After many long days and nights, we went from a rough concept in July 2002 to the first day of nursing classes in August 2003. We didn't know that you aren't supposed to create an academic program that fast; anyone familiar with academia knows that *fast* isn't really part of their DNA. Our ignorance was not only bliss, but a blessing.

We built the program in six months, including finding a building to house the program. It was a heady, crazy time. Lots of LONG days and sleepless nights, but we pulled it off! Over eight years, the program supported students in obtaining their general education, nursing program prerequisites, and registered nurse education. It served more than 800 students leading to the **555** that graduated as nurses to care for the communities we served.

There were many twists and turns along the way in this program. I will tell you, even with being an adult student myself, I had no idea of the level of joy, angst, and trauma these nursing students would endure throughout the 18-month program. That's right – we accelerated the traditional program. Despite the challenges that arose, by the time the program ended in 2018, we had produced 555 new registered nurses to serve the community. In addition, the program was tuition-free, and employment agreements were not required. This was a community benefit program in the truest sense, designed to support its health and well-being.

The collaborative nursing program was so successful that the governor used it as a model to increase the supply of nurses statewide. A proud moment!

You might wonder what this story has to do with the joy of work. The story of the nursing program is a powerful example of how meaningful work can lead to joy and fulfillment. When we find work that is aligned with our values and passions, it can be a source of great satisfaction. This satisfaction can lead to many positive outcomes, including improved mental and physical health, increased productivity, and a stronger sense of purpose. As I was thinking about what I wanted all of you to know, I realized I find joy through meaningful work.

Work is defined as: **Work /wərk/** *Noun* (OxfordLanguages, 2023)

1. Activity involving mental or physical effort done in order to achieve a purpose or result.

2. A task or tasks to be undertaken, something a person or thing has to do.

Does that sound exciting to you? Me either. There is nothing about *JOY* in that definition, so we must create it ourselves. Meaningful work is purposeful and contributes to something greater than yourself, connecting with your values, piquing your interest, and engaging your moral compass. This can be as simple as helping a customer find the right product or as complex as working on a project that will change the world. When you find meaning in your work, it becomes more than just a job, it becomes a calling. I found meaning in the nursing program. While not a clinician, I still had an impact on the care my community members received from the excellent nurses created through this program.

Do you remember the energy and enthusiasm you brought to work each day when you were starting out in your career?

Joy at work may look different for each person, but there's no denying it has an important role in our lives. Joy can be felt through feeling a sense of accomplishment and satisfaction from our hard work. It also comes from lightening up the monotony of tasks with humor or banter among coworkers or doing something meaningful we enjoy. Joy at work excites us about going to the office, whether in-person or virtual and encourages us to feel energized by the challenges and opportunities we face. Remember, joy isn't only found outside of work activities - it can be found within them too!

We all know the saying,

Choose a job you love and you'll never have to work
a day in your life ~ Confucius

Have you ever stopped to think about what that actually means? It's not just about liking your job, but finding meaning in your work. When you find meaning in your career, joy naturally follows.

In an increasingly hectic world, meaningful work can provide a respite. It allows us to focus on something that truly matters and provides the satisfaction of achieving tangible results at the end of the day. In addition, a work ethic focused on meaningful pursuits can provide a deeper connection to our work, increasing productivity, mental clarity, and even physical well-being.

Meaningful work can also be a great source of career growth opportunities, as it allows us to continuously learn and grow in our tasks and add value to future projects. By investing in meaningful work, we can create aspects of our job that are above and beyond, creating long-term job stability. Ultimately, engaging in meaningful work leads to greater mental well-being by providing a challenge with purpose – something we all strive for daily!

There are a number of factors that contribute to meaningful work. First, it is important to find work that is aligned with our values. Values are the principles and beliefs guiding your actions and decisions, while passions are the things you are most excited and motivated to do. By identifying your values and passions, you can begin to find work that aligns with them. This can include finding a job in a field you are passionate about or working for a company that aligns with your values. This means finding work that we believe in and are passionate about. When we are working on something that we care about, it is much easier to find joy in our work.

Once you have identified your values and passions, the next step is to find ways to incorporate them into your work. This can be done by taking on projects or tasks that align with your values and passions or by finding ways to make your current work more meaningful. Meaningful work should challenge us. It should not be too easy, but it should not be too difficult either. For example, if you are passionate about environmental conservation, you may seek opportunities to work on sustainability projects within your company. If your values include helping others, you may seek volunteer opportunities within your organization or community. That's what I have done since the nursing program. When work seemed tedious, I engaged with my community by sitting on multiple community and nonprofit boards that feed my soul. When we are challenged, we are forced to grow and learn. This growth can lead to a sense of accomplishment and satisfaction.

Third, meaningful work should connect us to others. We should feel like we are part of a team and that we are making a difference in the world. When we feel connected to others, it can help us to feel more fulfilled. You can do this by building solid relationships with your colleagues, fostering a culture of respect and collaboration, and maintaining open lines of communication with your supervisor. A positive work environment can help create a sense of community and belonging, leading to greater job satisfaction and overall well-being. In our remote, post-pandemic world, these relationships are more important than ever and require intentionality to create.

Finally, meaningful work should be rewarding. This means that it should provide us with a sense of purpose and satisfaction. When we find work that is rewarding, it can make us feel like we are making a difference in the world. Think about a time when you were really focused and engaged in a task at work. Maybe it was a particularly challenging project, or perhaps it was something you were passionate about. Either way, chances are good that you felt a sense of joy while doing it. That's because meaningful work leads to happiness at work. When we care about what we're doing and feel like our efforts are making a difference, we can't help but be joyful.

The story of the nursing program is a powerful example of how all of these factors came together to create meaningful work for me. The program was aligned with the values of the people who created it. It challenged us and helped us all grow. It connected me to others and made us all feel like we were making a difference in the world. It was rewarding, providing a sense of purpose and satisfaction.

If you are looking for joy and fulfillment in your work, I encourage you to consider the factors that contribute to meaningful work. When you find work aligned with your values, that challenges you, connects you to others and is rewarding, you are more likely to find joy in your work.

In addition to the factors mentioned above, there are a number of other things that can contribute to finding joy in work. These include:

- Having a clear sense of purpose. When you know why you are doing your work, it is easier to find meaning in it.

- Working with people you enjoy. When you enjoy the people you work with, it makes work more enjoyable.

- Having a flexible work schedule. A flexible work schedule can help you to balance your work and personal life, which can lead to greater satisfaction.

- Having opportunities for growth and development. When you have opportunities to learn and grow, it can help you to feel more fulfilled in your work.

Questions to ask yourself:

1. What is the meaning of joy at work?

2. How can I find meaningful work that leads to joy?

3. What are some tips for creating a joyful workspace for myself and others around me?

4. How can I bring more joy into my current work situation?

5. What are some things to avoid if I want to maintain a joyful attitude at work?

If you are not currently finding joy in your work, don't despair. There are several things you can do to change that. Start by identifying what is important to you and what you are passionate about. Then, look for work that aligns with your values and interests. Once you have found a job that you are interested in, make an effort to connect with your colleagues and build relationships. In the remote, post-pandemic world, we must be more intentional about making connections. Finally, don't be afraid to ask for help or make changes if you are unhappy with your current situation.

To bring this message home, my best friend, who is like another sister to me, was diagnosed with breast cancer in the summer of 2018. Her treatment plan required a double mastectomy, chemotherapy, and radiation. Imagine my shock and amazement when I realized that some of her nurses were graduates of the nursing program! They are now well-tenured in their careers and provided excellent care for her. In partnership with her incredible doctors, those nurses saved her life; she is cancer-free and THRIVING! I recognize that this is not a common occurrence. However, I am so proud to have been a part of a program that ultimately impacted not only the community I love, but someone that I love.

For me, that one life was worth the pain and angst required to create the nursing program, and I found meaning in that work. So, my desire for you is that you find it too.

Finding joy at work can be a challenging task, but it is possible by focusing on meaningful work that aligns with your values and passions and allows you to make a positive impact. You can find greater joy and fulfillment in the workplace by identifying your values and passions, incorporating them into your work, and creating a positive and supportive work environment. Lastly, remember that finding joy at work is a process that takes time, but with persistence, you will find your way to it.

Anette Smith

Anette Smith is a seasoned consultant with over 15 years of experience in the nonprofit sector. She is passionate about helping organizations achieve their goals and make a difference in their communities. Anette has a proven track record of success in a variety of roles, including the following.

Strategic planning: She has helped organizations develop clear and concise plans that align with their mission, vision, and values. Organizational development: She has helped organizations improve their culture, communication, and collaboration. Leadership development: She has helped leaders develop their skills and abilities to be more effective. Coaching: She has provided one-on-one coaching to help individuals achieve personal and professional goals. Diversity, equity, and inclusion: She has helped organizations create more inclusive workplaces. She offers diverse skills to help people and organizations achieve their goals. Here are some additional details about Anette's experience: She is a certified DiSC(c) Coach. She will soon be an accredited coach through the International Coaching Federation (2024). Anette is highly motivated and results-oriented, passionate about making a difference. Did we also mention she is an obsessed Labradoodle dog mom? Bixley, her annoying coworker, likes to join in on Zoom calls.

Connect with Anette at www.impactgroupenterprises.com.

CHAPTER 5

Make Joy Your Work!

by Chineme Noke

Part 1: Promote and Facilitate a Positive, Energetic, Joyful Workforce!

I had been given the job three years earlier, as the Corporation was looking for a changemaker – a good legal mind as well as proven experience and leadership skills in their new Principal Lawyer, Department of Law and Corporate Services. It had been widely recognized by the Corporate Leadership Team that I managed to turn the whole legal department around within my first year of working there.

When I began, the staff were very unhappy and, consequently, they were not very productive. Their surroundings were not at all uplifting or conducive to serious, corporate, legal representation. The equipment was always breaking down and was totally out of date. I found that just walking into the department was unpleasant; I still describe the energy

I felt as being like wading through mud. It did not take a genius to work out that the staff felt ignored, unvalued, and totally unloved.

I knew immediately that the whole department needed a complete overhaul, so I had to be rather creative in persuading the powers that be that organisational productivity was absolutely and inextricably linked to having a joyful workforce.

I decided to prove this by undertaking a Post Graduate Diploma (PGD) in Management Studies, at the Corporation's expense, simply to conduct an academic, empirical study of the workings of the Legal Department as my dissertation. The main hypothesis was: Does Morale (state of mind, etc.) play any role in staff productivity? Or is it all down to Motivation (e.g. pay)? At the end of the year-long program, I was awarded an A for the PGD overall, and an A for the Dissertation itself.

I presented my findings to the Corporate Leadership Team. The Legal Department had had such a bad reputation that they were extremely happy to see that someone was actually taking an interest in them, and was willing to dig deep to ascertain what the real problems were!

I was given the go-ahead to spruce up the offices, procure essential equipment such as photocopiers etc., all while making the work environment fun and elevating the energy and productivity levels of the staff. It was not a mammoth task; things such as having each member of the team prepare for and chair our weekly meetings, and having meetings somewhere other than in the office, e.g. at the coffee shop next door were just two things that were implemented immediately to ensure my staff were fully involved in the running of their workplace.

In a truly short space of time, I had changed the whole attitude of my team; we began to win corporate and national recognition and awards for our innovative solutions for complex legal problems, and, most importantly, my staff worked happily as a team - as I believe work should always be.

I knew that the key lay in HOW to draw out the best from my staff/ team members in the workplace. It was instinctive; however, to convince the Corporate Leadership Board of my convictions, I set out to prove it with my dissertation - my academic study.

I believe that joy and purpose should extend naturally to the workplace. It should be woven into the *cultural and leadership* fabric of every organization, given that the employees spend a good portion of their time at work.

Work environments and culture inevitably evolve over time and can, of course, be adapted or can experience positive change if the members of the team are all moving in a similar direction towards a common goal.

Discussing leadership, John C. Maxwell stated that, "A leader is one who knows the way, goes the way, and shows the way."

John Quincy Adams said, "If your actions inspire others to dream more, learn more, do more, and become more, you are a leader."

I believe that if you lead with kindness, inclusivity, and example, it will engender trust, loyalty, increased, purposeful effort and productivity. Plus, an essential ingredient in the cultural mix is making work FUN!

When measuring the impact of different working conditions on output at the Western Electric Hawthorne Works in Chicago from 1924 to 1927, my research revealed that variations in output were not caused by changing physical conditions or material rewards, but partly *by the experiments themselves*.

The special treatment required by experimental participation convinced workers that management had a particular interest in them. This raised morale, which led to increased happiness and productivity soared.

The term 'Hawthorne Effect' is now widely used to refer to the behaviour-modifying effects of being the subject of social investigation and feeling like part of a team with their supervisors, regardless of the context of the investigation. The study also concluded that supervisory style greatly affected worker productivity and inspired Professor George Elton Mayo (1880-1949) and his Harvard colleagues to develop the Human Relations Movement between 1924 and 1932.

Many academic studies since then have shown that human productivity is increased or decreased by the way in which we are all treated. They have shown the evolutionary process that has taken place in the management of people. We now know that we can get the best out of people by treating everyone with respect and having regard for their feelings, thoughts, and aspirations. I consider it imperative that this knowledge is utilised in the workplace.

As the late, great Dr. Maya Angelou so rightly said, "People will forget what you say, they will forget what you do, but they will always remember the way you made them feel."

Part 2: Maintain the Joy by Never Allowing Any Injustice to Go Unchallenged.

At the beginning of my 3rd year at the same organisation, the Head of Law was to be away from his post for at least six months and the two Principal Lawyers were invited to apply to act up while he was away. I was literally doing the job anyway and so I applied, as did the other male, Principal Lawyer.

The main criterion was that the applicant must be a fully qualified lawyer - an attorney or barrister. We were both interviewed, and my client Directors were just as stunned as I was when he got the job instead of me, given our skills, experience, and impact.

I had been in similar situations many times before in my legal career but, given all of my highly commended work within the legal department, it was clear to me that yet again, one or more "isms" was being played out. I challenged the decision, and the process at the time was that there had to be an Internal Review prior to taking the matter to a court of law. I, therefore, requested all the relevant documentation to scrutinize in minute detail in preparation for my appeal.

Not only did I discover that my opponent did NOT have the relevant, required legal qualification (which meant he should not even have been a Principal Lawyer, let alone be shortlisted for the top position), but the panel discussions had involved the fact that my daughter has a disability! Therefore, not only was it a case of Sexism and Racism, but it also involved Disability discrimination!

I remember the feeling of being completely let down by those involved, particularly given the magnitude of what I had achieved in the organisation in such a short space of time. Due to my findings, my noted experience, and my previous legal precedents against discriminatory practices within other corporations, they did NOT want this matter going into the public domain. I, therefore, agreed to a six-figure settlement and went happily on my way.

As I had already made the decision to leave the corporate life to spend more quality time with my daughter, it was as if the Universe had found a way to assist me. My team and client Directors were reassured that I was ready to move on to my next calling as we had all successfully achieved what I had set out to do in the Legal Department. I felt very proud to see that my team had learned the essence of the joy of work and was confident that this would continue.

My final lesson is that you should never allow an injustice to remain unchallenged; otherwise, it will play on your mind and continue to interfere with your future sense of justice and joy, simply because you did not take the appropriate action to seek closure. Always keep in mind the adage that, 'we work to live, not live to work.' Therefore, ensure that you strive for and jealously maintain the joy within your work.

Chineme Noke

Chineme Noke has a long career as a lawyer, success coach, and international speaker. She is an award-winning author for her book *Special Hidden Talents* and has multiple Amazon #1 bestsellers. Her expertise is in all round Obstacle and Challenge obliteration - with ease. She does this by dealing effectively with what she calls the mountains and molehills that success seekers encounter in their daily lives, by following her seven-step action plan from her first published book, *There is No Time like the Present to Create Your Future.* She is the founder of the Unstoppable Bizpreneurship program and the Unstoppable Shepreneurs private Facebook® group, as well as the author of her next publication, *Unstoppable Shepreneurs: Become An Emboldened and Empowered Woman, Live An Exceptional Life and Leave Your Legacy.*

Connect with Chineme on LinkedIn @chinemenoke.

Raise Your Voice

by Diane Davidson

I love singing. It's the ultimate expression of who I am, how I view the world, and how I feel about everything. It brings me joy and people tell me it brings them joy as well. I've made a living with my voice and would be content if that's all I ever did. I knew this very early on in my life.

Being the tallest, I was always placed in the back of the classroom, and with low vision I was frequently deep in my own world. In third grade, we started each day facing the flag with our hands over our hearts reciting the Pledge of Allegiance and singing the National Anthem. Unlike the other kids' rote performances, I wanted to improve every time I sang it. After all, it was my favorite subject! One morning during the Anthem, feeling particularly confident, I raised my voice a bit toward the end with my newly discovered operatic soprano sound, "O'er the land of the free-eee…" and when I nailed the high note, the class stopped singing and abruptly looked back at me.

The giggles started erupting as I sank down on my desk and tucked my face behind my folded arms. I could hear the teacher approaching with her heels pounding loudly on the floor. When she arrived at my desk, I looked up hoping she'd be kind, but instead she taunted me with a sarcastic, challenging tone, "Would you like to sing in front of the whole class, Diane?" I nervously declined while making a mental note, 'don't ever share your talents and skills or you'll be ridiculed and humiliated in front of everyone.' It took me years to trust others enough to bring that voice out again.

Aunt Ruth bought our family a piano when I was six and I took lessons at Evansville College. I struggled with the traditional approach because it was hard to see the tiny notes on the sheet music, and I felt so limited when the strict teacher covered up my hands (apparently, you weren't allowed to look down at the keys). I wanted to quit, but at nine years old, my parents arranged for me to have lessons with a laid-back jazz pianist instead. The smooth sounds of the chord progressions opened my eyes to a whole new world of possibilities. Finally free to fully express myself, I could improvise and play the music that had been streaming in my mind all along. Piano was my new thing, so with my six-year-old sister singing, and my seven-year-old brother on bass guitar, we started a family band.

Dad was our manager and we played for tens of thousands of people at festivals, corporate events, and private parties. We were the REAL Partridge Family, working and making great money. At fourteen, twelve, and eleven years old, we had a weekly gig with a Big Band at an elegant showroom lounge. One night someone from the food and beverage commission came in and escorted us out of the club. Knowing what might be coming, Dad said, "What's wrong?" The man said factually, "This establishment serves alcohol, and these musicians are underage." Dad explained that he was with us at every gig, and of course we didn't drink any alcohol. As if it was an assigned, mandatory, unwanted task the man blurted out, "They can't work here!" and briskly departed. What a moment that was. We started calling ourselves "Pros" realizing that by getting paid and now being fired was the definition of being "professional" musicians. It was epic!

One day at lunch, I was practicing piano so I could accompany the singers in the upcoming musical auditions, when my high school choir teacher walked in the classroom. I stopped playing and waved hello. Trying not to disturb, he motioned for me to continue, then scratched his head and started looking around the room for something. Puzzled, he walked over to where I was seated on the bench and questioned, "Diane, was that you singing?" I said bashfully, "Yes." He disbelievingly exclaimed, "I didn't know you could sing like that; you should audition for the musical." I giggled, "I'd rather just play piano in the orchestra pit." He insisted, "I think you should audition to sing." I got the leading role as Nellie Forbush in South Pacific.

I loved everything about musical theater, rehearsing, memorizing lines, getting the timing and pacing with other actors, being directed and coached, and singing onstage with a full orchestra. I found my calling.

I started taking voice lessons and continued getting leading roles, placing 1st in state vocal competitions, performing in theme parks, and getting feedback that I had a shot at a real music career, so I decided to major in vocal performance at Indiana University.

My parents had been saving up for college and I wanted to contribute so, at seventeen, I got a part-time job making outbound calls selling a seasonal coupon book sponsored by a local business club. I was quickly promoted and coached new employees on improving their voice tone while reading the script.

One day during lunch, the FBI showed up and took me aside. They wanted me to spy on my boss who had been embezzling from business sponsors all over the Midwest. Our building was partially leased with some suites still under construction, and they tasked me with searching the building looking for the money. I was scared, but I used my acting skills to keep it together when he was around, then when he left, I went into action.

Two floors up in an empty office, I saw some drywall that had been cut in a square and put back. I pushed it open and in between two steel studs I saw a green metal utility box, so I pulled it out and opened it. It was full of cash with a pistol sitting on top! I quietly closed it, squeezed it back in the wall, and called the FBI. They told me to go for a coffee. When I returned, there were three black cars in front. They had my boss handcuffed and were walking him out of the building and down the steps. He looked at me as they put him in the back seat, but he didn't seem to suspect anything. I went home and nonchalantly told my parents that I was a spy for the FBI. At first, they just laughed. But then... well, you can imagine.

The next year I auditioned and was accepted at IU to study opera. I paid down my tuition singing jazz at night and during the summers I worked as a singing waitress at dinner theaters in Florida. One night, with a full house in West Palm Beach, I had just balanced and served sixteen fruit-heavy tall hurricane cocktails, without spilling a drop and had made it to the stage with precision timing to sing my big solo. I was seated in the dark on a bar stool, with a narrow spotlight on my face, and was nearing the end of Olivia Newton John's tender song of love lost, "I Honestly Love You." Suddenly, with a loud voice, a customer in the front row demanded, "Diane, where's my Sanka?!" With a startled jump, and thousands of quips at the tip of my tongue, I knew full well I had to ignore her, so I continued. Gathering all the self-control I could muster, staying in character, tears glistening and the spotlight closing in on my eyes, I whispered the last words of the song, "I love you." I stood up, carried my stool with me and gracefully exited the stage. What's the old saying, the show must go on? I shook it off the best I could, but seriously… how disrespectful!

Back to work with a round of appetizers, another group number, then the main course of a prime rib dinner. I had just placed the twelfth plate at my sixteen top, and the lady two seats down started screaming at the top of her lungs, "this potato's bad, this potato's bad!" Come on!!! I thought people came for the show, not the gourmet potato. I mean, it's in foil, people! You don't know what's in there until you cut it open; it's hit or miss on the black spots. Honestly, I'd just about had it with these rude, often non-tipping customers. At that moment, something inside me just snapped. I picked up that potato, started spanking it and said, "Bad Potato, Bad Potato!" I put it back on her plate and said, "Ma'am, if that potato gives you any more trouble, you let me know!" As she gasped, I straightened up, turned around, and walked away. My walk turned into a sprint as I realized, "I AM SO FIRED!" and ran to the kitchen for another potato. Thank goodness she was laughing when I approached, "Thanks, Diane, you are so funny, my favorite waitress, you're just hilarious!" Firing averted.

One semester short of graduating from IU, I was offered a contract to sing in a vocal quartet on cruise ships. I didn't even question whether I should stay and finish the last semester of my degree because I was going to do what I was going to college to learn how to do. No brainer!

It was a quick ramp-up having been contracted to be onboard in only six weeks performing in the showroom lounge. We had our own music director that wrote our arrangements out by hand on lined staff paper, as this was before everyone had computers. The five of us worked around the clock to create and produce four 60-minute shows including vocal and orchestra music arrangements, dialogue, stage blocking, choreography, dance numbers, costuming, etc. Our four shows included a Broadway Review, Country Show, Pop Show, and Manhattan Transfer Show. Then we each built our own solo acts where we'd perform with a jazz trio in the cabaret lounge. It all seemed impossible, but we did it!

We loaded up our costumes and flew to New York. I had heard the ship was enormous, super luxurious, and had been rated the world's best cruise line by multiple travel magazines, but when we pulled up, I couldn't believe my eyes. The massive Royal Viking Sea, with the lines' sea eagle logo emblazoned on the ship's funnel, was fourteen stories high and over two football fields long. My head was spinning as we boarded, and I was escorted to my luxury stateroom where a crystal bucket was icing a bottle of champagne.

We had a few hours before we sailed, so our on-board boss, the cruise director, gave us a tour of the ship. It took weeks before I could wean off the "you are here map" to navigate the ship. The showrooms were spectacular with bronze and white marble accents. We met the band who were from Poland on a government contract. All exquisite musicians as they were required to play at least ten instruments each at a master level to get the job. At home they were all university music professors. It's a good thing because they had to read our handwritten charts!

Following the tour, the cruise director arranged for some champagne, and we went outside to sail away. We gathered with the band as they played Dixieland Music and for the first time ever, we stood as a team on the glossy wood plank promenade deck, beaming with radiant smiles and bursting with hearty laughter as we took in our surroundings. With language as a barrier, there was a joyful silence between us, but there was a knowing that all had a lifetime of diligent studying, practicing, and preparing. Each of us had passionately pursued the same dream and finally here we stood, coming from all over the world to enjoy this amazing work experience together and it was going to be extraordinary.

When the sound of the ship's horns broke the moment with a long earthshaking rumble and thousands of colorful streamers exploded in the air, our hearts swelled with a sense of great accomplishment. So, we raised our champagne flutes and as the ship separated from the dock and floated out to sea we toasted to the journey of a lifetime.

After cruising all five oceans on the planet plus the arctic circle and going all the way around the world visiting ports-of-call on six continents, at twenty-three years old, I moved to California and began my career as a recording artist, voice-over talent, and jingle singer. My partner and I built a studio and began producing commercials, corporate videos, and feature films. He was the engineer and producer, and I ran every other aspect of the business including producing, creative, human resources, marketing, casting, talent coaching and development. After fourteen years, we sold the studio, and I was ready for a new adventure.

My parents who had successful careers in the finance business suggested that I interview with their company. I laughed, "Singer to lending? That's quite a leap, don't you think? Seriously, what would I do, exactly?" Encouragingly they continued, "Think about it honey, you've got a lot of skills." "Like what, singing their jingle?," I joked. They went on to name a few things I had done at my studio that would be considered valuable skills in the corporate arena which convinced me to at least do an interview.

I got the job and my boss explained that they were starting a new department with a hiring strategy of selecting people for their positive attitudes and providing industry specific skills in a three-week training. He thought I was a good fit for the team because I had built and run my own business, which meant I had the needed start-up entrepreneurial skills. And since I was a performer, I could be a fantastic trainer with my stage presence and comfort in front of an audience. I had no idea!

The first team meeting was about aligning the mission, vision, and values to behaviors. This was a new idea to me, and it immediately made perfect sense. We talked about how to teach that "Can-Do" attitude and how to create a WOW training experience. I immediately had ideas, but I was embarrassed to share in front of everyone. Yet another voice inside said trust your boss, he's been 100% supportive, he took a chance on hiring you, now speak up!

I asked for a meeting and began to share, "I understand we want our learners to embrace and exhibit the behaviors of our core values. What if we wrote songs, and everyone sang the words of our values and behaviors? It'd be so much more memorable and engaging than those posters on the walls. Like how singing along with catchy commercials makes you want to try products, and how joining in with praise songs helps you memorize scripture. What do you think?" He tentatively nodded, "Yeah, we could do that." I have a song in my head, you want to hear it? He snickered a little uncomfortably under his breath, but with an open mind replied, "Ok, yeah go ahead."

I stood up and started beatboxing like I did when I shared a jingle idea with a potential client. It was totally natural for me, but he awkwardly smiled and laughed. I was tapping my hands on my tummy and chest and singing a big boomy bass line when he enthusiastically jumped up and joined in with me. He started clapping with the beat and dancing around, and we were totally in sync when I belted out the song ala C+C Music Factory! At the end he applauded and exclaimed, "Yes, let's do it! We are doing it!"

The songs were memorized, and core values embraced. They even sang as they tossed their caps at graduation. When our team walked through the call centers to do follow-up coaching, they stood up, singing and dancing with fists pumping! A WOW experience indeed!

I had been doing onboarding and sales training for a year, so when a management and leadership trainer position opened, I had some skills that would transfer nicely. My new boss set me up for success by sending me to be certified in Ken Blanchard's SLII™, and Steven Covey's 7 Habits of Highly Effective People. I was so excited to share that powerful learning and deliver those classes to hundreds of employees and managers across the entire company. This was my new passion. I could hardly believe I had found work, in addition to the music business, that was so purposeful and satisfying.

When that company was sold in 1999, I was contracted back independently, which launched my current leadership development consulting practice and I've been producing songs and videos, facilitating and training, mentoring and coaching, public speaking, performing, and singing ever since.

I must share that I also experience something called imposter syndrome. That inner voice that says I'm not enough, no matter what I've done, what experiences I've had, or what education I've accumulated. Can you relate? Do you have moments of self-doubt that sometimes hold you back? It's like an old song replaying in your head that questions everything. "Are you sure you know what you're doing? You're in over your head, what makes you think you can do that?"

We need to listen to the new song that says, "I am enough, I have the experience, I'm the real deal." Just remember what my parents said, "Honey, you've got skills!" Sometimes we need other people to see that for us, to open our eyes and show us how our skills can transfer to other wonderful opportunities. Then we trust those voices, move forward, and enjoy the journey.

I believe the joy of work is about doing what you love, growing personally and professionally, and most importantly, surrounding yourself with people that encourage you to confidently, and ever so boldly, RAISE YOUR VOICE!

Diane Davidson

Diane Davidson is a leadership development instructor and coach in Roseville, a suburb of Sacramento, California's state capital. She started her own practice in 1999 and is Principal of Diane Davidson Consulting, is an Instructor at UC Davis Continuing and Professional Education, a Senior Consultant with JD Thompson & Associates, a certified Marshall Goldsmith Stakeholder Centered Coach, and a Channel Partner with The Ken Blanchard Companies, certified in SLII™.

With over four decades of experience in the public, private and non-profit sectors, among numerous industries, locally, regionally, and internationally, Diane understands the challenges of ever-changing work environments, including the need to develop new supervisors and managers who are recently hired or promoted from within organizations.

Diane supports employee engagement and leadership development strategic plans by helping her clients identify gaps in specific competencies, skills and behaviors among managers and leaders. With a phased approach, she designs and delivers customized training programs in half or full-day modules that are implemented over 6-9-12 months. Delivered in cohorts or as standalone courses, some topics include Giving & Receiving Feedback, Managing Change, Team Engagement, Problem Solving, and Communication Skills. Diane offers coaching for public speaking events with her presentation skills model entitled ROCK STAR Guide To Success!©

As a professional entertainer, Diane is known to deliver very interactive and entertaining sessions in person and virtually on Zoom. Using relevant, relatable, and sometimes humorous stories and examples, Diane has the connectability to create a safe learning environment and quickly engage various learning styles.

Connect with Diane at https://dianedavidson.me.

CHAPTER 7

Joy, Immeasurable Joy!

by Jen M. Clarke

Finding joy in helping my clients launch and grow their businesses has made me feel like a Super Bowl Winning kind of Business Coach! One of my greatest touch-down winning moments was when, recently, a single mother of four children was about to lose her home and become homeless, again. She had been homeless, after a divorce during the worldwide lockdowns in 2020, and was on the verge of being homeless again, three years later. It was at this point that she reached out to me for business coaching. I started coaching her with her business right away, due to the urgency of her situation. In exactly one week, she enrolled her first high ticket, high paying client and then proceeded to enroll five clients over the next few weeks. Immediately, the trajectory of her situation changed for the better! She had mentioned that her bank app was always showing projections in the negative; however, now her bank app was showing her financial projections to be in the positive. This has brought me so much elation and joy in my work.

To have the privilege of helping those in difficult situations see success in a short period of time and then to be able to help many more people through your work is one of the greatest joys ever! This type of joy is immeasurable. With my business coaching, the client followed the steps needed to work their way out of their dire circumstance to a winning victory in their business. Thus providing a brighter future for themselves and their family. The most rewarding aspect of helping my clients build their businesses is when the client is in a situation that seems hopeless and their whole life is changed in a short time frame. This is the amazing legacy that I want to continue to build for many clients and their families, as well as for my own family.

Over most of my life, my husband and I have donated tens of thousands of hours in volunteer time and countless resources. We continued giving to others to the point that it had put us into our own difficult financial situation. We worked for non-profit organizations and after many years, I realized that running charities are for the wealthy and not for those that are in need themselves. It's difficult to give out of one's own lack and need. The family that built the non-profit charitable organization that we worked for were very wealthy and I realized that I was believing something that wasn't true. I was always taught, while growing up, that it's better to give than receive; however, I interpreted it as it's best to give and to not receive. I had planned and hosted numerous live events, retreats, workshops, seminars, and would never ask for anything more than the cost of the event. We would often pay for a retreat weekend for others and would pay for others out of our own family's budget. Often going into debt to give others great experiences. I wouldn't even take-up an offering or ask for donations for myself, only if we had a guest speaker that would expect an offering or donation for their speaking engagement. This caused our family to suffer financially, at times, and even go into debt in the tens of thousands. I was recently wondering why I did this and realized it's false humility, which is pride. Believing the lie that you need to give until you have less than nothing left for your own family, so you become the ones needing charitable support is a type of pride. This type of pride that says, "I can give and give and never expect or need anything in return," severely affects one's own financial security and future. There's a better way to give. Giving out of your overflow of abundance from finding joy in your work that is profitable is a much better way to give. It brings monetary abundance and enables one to have a good impact toward others in our world.

I have a huge vision to bring healing to this world by changing economic situations for individuals, families, and communities. I have a strong sense of urgency to bring clean drinking water to many areas of need in the world, to reduce world hunger with organic farming, and to also help orphans, widows, and those that are in impoverished situations. When you have a thriving business that is making a profit, then you can direct the overflow and abundance to areas that are in the most need. It is better to give from a place of prosperity, than to create a detrimental situation for yourself and your family. It's better to create a sustainable financial position whereby you can give on a continual basis that has a long-term effect on truly building a legacy for your family and for other families around the world. The priority we have on this earth is to provide for our own family first and then to make a huge difference in the lives of others. I had my priorities in the opposite order for most of my life and didn't realize how detrimental it was to our family. My husband and I wanted to see the others in this world healed, saved, and be provided for and to be part of making it happen. However, it was being done out of our financial lack, which created enormous debt, rather than doing it in a better way by helping others out of the overflow of our abundance. By launching and growing a suc- cessful business it allows a consistent and sustainable source of income to provide for one's own family and for charitable endeavors. Creating a significant impact for good in this world at home and in the areas that we have a strong sense of calling to make a difference for the better.

As a person who loves to give and be supportive to others and having given in abundance, even when it was difficult and caused financial hardship for my own family, I now realize that it is important to allow others to contribute to their well-being in whatever area that we are wanting to see them thrive in. When we allow others to invest in their own lives, with some assistance if necessary, they will value it more and put in the effort to see their own success in that particular area. The best way, that I know, to empower people to take responsibility and ownership in their lives is to offer them my business coaching. To help them launch their business as quickly as possible. Business coaching has been some of the most joyful work that I've been able to do. I've coached my clients away from giving their products or services for free or for very little, and then seeing them start to be valued for what they offer to the world. The most joyous elation is when I help someone, who is a good person with great values and integrity, become wealthy in order to do good in this world.

The true purpose and joy that is found in our work is to release our treasures, gifting, talents, and calling to the world, making an impact for the good of others. The result of releasing our gifts to the world, for an exchange of energy in the way of financial increase, will preferably result in freedom! The focus needs to be on financial freedom, time freedom, and freedom to be who you were called and meant to be at birth. If you are able to fully release your gifts, talents, and treasures and have fulfilling work by helping others for their benefit and for the benefit of others. Releasing all of your gifts and talents, while experiencing total freedom in life, would be the ultimate joy in your work!

A significant key to experiencing freedom, joy, and fulfillment in our calling are our thoughts, both our conscious and subconscious thoughts. We need to take a very real look and evaluate what our sub-conscious is saying, so that we can get rid of the negative thoughts and replace them with thoughts that will focus on and bring us to our ulti-mate goals in life, ensuring they will be accomplished. The reason why positive thinking alone doesn't always work is because our subcon-scious thoughts are truly what is making the decisions in our lives and running our actions. Our subconscious thoughts need to be changed for the positive to fulfill our desired goals in our lives. It's important to get out all of the negative thoughts through journaling and speaking about what you want to see happen, while feeling the elation of joy with the accomplishment of our life's purpose! We must first become the per-son that we want to be when we have everything that we want to see happen. Once we become the person that has what we truly want to see happen, then we have a higher potential to make it a reality in our lives!

Many people don't know what they are supposed to do for their work or career. I've heard grown adults say that they have no gifts, no talents, and nothing to offer. They are believing a lie about them-selves and that those that think that they have nothing to offer, most likely, have the most to offer. They just haven't had the opportunity to discover and develop the great gifts that they have to offer the world. I struggled with these very same thoughts for many years and now recognize that I coach my clients to succeed and thrive in numerous areas of specialty. It brings me joy to coach my clients to realize their gifts and talents, as it reveals the gifts and talents that I have at the same time. This is beyond anything I ever thought that I could actually do in this life. I've often thought of creating many small businesses, in almost every niche that my clients are in. I would want to do this just to show that a successful business can be created in a very short period of time, in that area of business. I think this would be a fun challenge, however, staying in my zone of genius is the ideal focus for maximum success. I will most likely build more businesses in a few other niches, just to know that I have released as many of the gifts, talents, and treasures that I have to offer this world. To benefit the legacy that is being created for our children.

Paving the way for my children to become successful in their lives is another ultimate joy. The legacy that is created for our children is a powerful motivator. Finding the balance for creating the environment for our children to invest and contribute to the legacy that they are inheriting from their parents is of utmost importance. The children that have invested in the legacy that their parents created will more likely value that legacy. It is important that their own gifts, talents, and treasures be utilized to the fullest within the legacy business that they have received. When a generation has to start from scratch, rather than build upon what their parents have built, it can make their lives more difficult. The current economic situation that our nation is experiencing could potentially turn around and thrive, if more families decide to work together to invest in businesses, to create a prosperous family legacy. The completion of a university or college degree doesn't guarantee a successful career in our current economic environment. Having a business where our children can utilize their gifts and talents in a significant way will benefit the children and others that are in their sphere of influence. The children can then stand on the foundation that their parents built, rather than starting from the beginning, once again. Training our children to have a good work ethic is important, especially teaching them to work smarter and more efficiently and building upon what their parents have created can bring more time freedom and financial freedom for each generation. Encouraging gratitude and an appreciation for what our children are receiving can make the transition from one generation to the next a more enjoyable experience for everyone involved.

The greatest joy with our work can be providing for our family and creating freedom through a financial legacy that benefits our future generations. Freedom is a value that is deeply ingrained into me, so much so that the plans that my husband and I have are to enjoy freedom and to have significant work that brings financial freedom to my clients at the same time. Creating a business where I can help others create time freedom, financial freedom, and generational freedom for good people that will have a good impact in this world, with their success, is a primary focus of my life's vision. The joy of work eventually leads to retirement and then it's the joy of fulfillment and freedom knowing that every gift, talent, and treasure that's inside of us has been utilized, to the maximum extent, for the benefit of so many people that we impacted in this world!

Jen M. Clarke

Jen M. Clarke has been a highly successful Business Coach to clients from all over the world. Jen is known for her expertise in helping Entrepreneurs and Business Owners enroll High Ticket clients within a day to a few weeks, on average! Jen M. Clarke has many years of experience building 6 and 7 figure businesses in various fields including financial planning, health and wellness, and retreats. Jen has also worked for not-for-profit charities and has organized events, retreats and conferences. She has established herself as a leading authority as a Business Coach.

Jen specializes in helping her clients attract and enroll high ticket clients. She has developed a proven method and step-by-step formula that coaches entrepreneurs to position themselves as the authority and experts in their field. Jen coaches her clients to communicate in a way that is highly effective to build their businesses very quickly when it's implemented.

Jen is known for her customized, engaging, and empowering Business Coaching. Jen is a speaker and has delivered keynote speeches at live events, retreats, workshops, seminars, conferences, and many other types of events, both in-person and online.

Jen M. Clarke has a commitment to excellence in helping her clients succeed, so they can reach their full potential! Jen's ultimate vision is for her and her clients to have a significant impact in this world to create a powerful legacy!

Connect with Jen at https://coachjenclarke.com.

Your Perfect Job Is Looking for You, Too!

by Jodi Santangelo-Ash

You've probably heard this quote from Confucius, "Do the work you love, and you'll never work again." Are you wondering if that quote will ever ring true for you?

Perhaps you're not quite feeling the joy at work these days and you get those dreaded Sunday night blues?

Maybe you're one of those people who...

- feels stuck in a dead-end job;

- has little to no work-life balance;

- is bored to tears doing work that's not fulfilling; or

- your joy at work is simply fading.

If that's you… you're not alone. But it doesn't have to be this way forever. The joy at work is real! You just haven't found it yet.

Read on to discover how I found purpose and passion in my work, learned to love Mondays again, and created a career and life I love (and you can, too).

My Story:

Loving my work started the morning I woke with a life-changing epiphany around the age of 42… I'll never forget that day. I had a huge aha, my Eureka moment, a signal from above, and I remember crying out to the universe…

"OH, MY GOSH! NOW I KNOW WHAT I WANT TO DO WITH THE REST OF MY LIFE"

You would have laughed had you been there. I was elated… I jumped out of bed and couldn't wait to get started on what was sure to be my purpose and passion for the rest of my life. I was as excited as a little kid on Christmas morning!

More on my AHA story in a minute… Here's the backstory…

It started in my early 30s. In what seemed like a so-called 'out-of-the-blue' situation, my life started to unravel and fall apart all at the same time: my marriage, my health, and even my corporate training job! A triple whammy!

Looking back, I can connect some of the dots to my life spiraling in a downward direction, but at that time I felt like I was blindsided and certainly never expected something like this could happen to me at such a young age.

I ended up staying in my pity party for quite some time. Too long, actually... blaming, complaining, and justifying my victim position, which of course made the situation worse. I got sicker and sicker with every 'poor me' thought!

Despite the negative black cloud looming over my head, I eventually landed another corporate training position.

The Turnaround:

After three or four years, I was still all alone and pretty darn sick. I took a deep dive into personal development, including reading the book and watching the movie *The Secret*. I played that movie morning and night until I could recite every single word. I hung on to the hope that if this message were true.... it meant that I had the ability to get out from underneath this hopelessness and despair and turn my life around.

If you're not familiar with *The Secret*, it's all about one of our universal laws called the Law of Attraction. The principles taught in this life-changing movie empower you to take back control of your life. Boy, did I ever need it.

A quick overview of the Law of Attraction–how and why it works:

The Law of Attraction is a universal principle that states you will attract to your life what you give your attention, energy, and focus to, positive or negative.

Because our thoughts and emotions are vibrational in nature, we attract the people, situations, and events that are similar in vibration. Just like a boomerang.

While you may not realize it, you've seen the Law of Attraction in action many times.

Think of a day when you were feeling happy and thankful and grateful…your day just kept getting better and better and you noticed more good things began showing up for you. You were on a roll and chalked it up to having a lucky day!

By the same token, you can probably recall a day you were feeling sad, ticked off, or frustrated and things seemed to get worse as the day went on. You might have uttered these words, "I should have stayed in bed." That was also the Law of Attraction in action!

What a powerful and empowering lesson that was for me to learn. I certainly didn't want any more of the crummy stuff I was getting.

After discovering that I had more control over my circumstances than ever thought possible, it was time to reclaim my power. I chose to live with deliberate intent, rather than by happenstance. I practiced those Law of Attraction principles very deliberately, as if my life depended on it. In fact, it did. I started by understanding that our thoughts and what we give our attention to create our reality. I stopped watching the negative news, surrounded myself with positive and uplifting people, and I only focused on what I wanted…. great health, a loving partner, and a meaningful and fulfilling career. And, over time, I attracted all of it. I met and married my 'ideal' guy, got a 100% healthy report, and…

Back to my aha story, that epiphany moment:

You see, having been a professional development and technical trainer for much of my career, and now having the empowerment tools to create a wonderful life for myself, it was in that moment that clarity came to me. I knew exactly what I wanted to do forever…. use my skills as a trainer, as well as my own life-changing proof, to help others make the positive changes they want in their life and career. What a perfect match! I wanted to become an evangelist for the message and principles of the Law of Attraction and could not wait to get rolling. But I didn't really know where to start.

It is said that you pick your destination, and the path will unfold. I had to trust that the Law of Attraction would work for me here, too, as long as I stayed focused on what I wanted.

I still had that corporate training position that I enjoyed and needed financially. While I loved the training aspect of my job and loved the people I worked with, I wasn't changing lives. I simply wasn't fulfilled at work and definitely wasn't living my newfound purpose. I wasn't passionate about the topics I was teaching. They didn't bring me joy.

So, in my spare time, I became a Certified Law of Attraction facilitator and Certified Canfield Success Principles Coach. I used all the tools in my toolbox (positive mindset, goals, affirmations, visualization, etc.) to take inspired action. One baby step led to another... I conducted small group talks sharing these life-changing principles, which led to larger seminars and conferences, which led to private coaching and, just like that, I was off and running. Eventually, about four years later, I attracted the freedom to leave my corporate job and venture out on my own.

And... that's what still fulfills me today. Through my speaking, coaching, and online training programs, I feel privileged to help people make the positive changes they want in their careers, relationships, health, abundance, and more. How lucky am I! Every day I celebrate that I found my dream job and get to live my purpose with passion!

So how will you know you're living your purpose and in your dream job?

You can tell by the way you feel. You have an inner guidance system that tells you when you are on course or off course by the amount of joy you are experiencing. For instance:

- You're passionate knowing you're using your unique gifts to create a life that is meaningful

- You wake up excited and can't wait to get started.... even on Mondays

- No one has to motivate you; you naturally feel motivated and inspired

- You feel alive and joyful

- You could do it all day and night and hardly look at the clock

- You're bursting with ideas and can hardly get to sleep

- You have the motivation to keep going even when times are tough

- You have high self-esteem and are genuinely happy for others' success

- You view success in terms of fulfillment and not just money

- You don't think of retirement

"Don't ask what the world needs. Ask what makes you come alive and go do it.
Because what the world needs is people who have come alive."
~Howard Thurman

So what makes you come alive? Self-Awareness is the key:

My story reveals how I found my Joy at Work. Awareness and opportunities sprang forth from my personal struggle.

What about your story? What life experiences can you draw upon, positive or negative, that may lead you to what you're truly meant to do?

Discovering YOU... what's important and what you love is the first step in discovering your purpose and how you are meant to express it in the world. Some people get hung up on their 'purpose.' But don't worry, purpose isn't something you need to make up; it's already there within you. Your job, through the process of self-awareness, is to uncover YOUR purpose.

As a coach, I have several reflection activities that I use with my clients to help them gain clarity and discover their ideal job. I've listed three of those below that I hope you'll find valuable. Find a little quiet time, grab a pen and paper or your favorite journal, and enjoy the process of discovering more of what's important to you!

1. Values: These things are important to me

Circle those words below that most resonate with you. Initially, you may be tempted to circle several. Then refining your list to 3 to 5 words will provide you with the most clarity and direction.

Possible Choices:

Accomplishment	Freedom	Loyalty
Challenge	Fun	Power
Community	Growth	Respect
Connection	Helping Others	Recognition

Control	Individuality	Safety
Contribution	Influence	Security
Creativity	Leadership	Spirituality

Sit with the words you chose for a period of time asking, "Is this really important to me?" These few words represent what is truly meaningful and fulfilling to you. You'll know if a job or career will bring you joy if it provides opportunities to include your values.

Pro Tip: Consider your words and what they mean to you when making career and other important decisions.

2. Clarity Activity

Draw a line down the middle of a piece of paper. In the left column, list 20 or more aspects of what you don't like about your current and past jobs. In the right column, list what you do like instead.

Pro Tip: The more you are able to identify and list what you don't like, the more clarity you'll birth about what you do like and do want in your ideal job. Here are a few examples:

Aspects of My Job I Don't Like	**What I Do Like Instead**
Don't feel challenged	Like to be challenged
Repetitive work	Variety
None of my values are being met	Enjoy living my values and feeling fulfilled

When complete, only focus on the 'do like' right column, because the Law of Attraction will match what you're giving your attention, energy, and focus to. Can you Imagine your dream job now… doing more of what you like to do and feeling fulfilled!?!

3. Things I Love to Do

Brainstorm a list of at least 20 things you absolutely LOVE doing:

Examples:

Teach

Travel

Photography

There is a myriad of ways to make money in any field that you love. How could you make a living doing one or more of the things you listed above – or how could you incorporate them more into your current job or business, so you feel more fulfilled?

Once you've done these three exercises, sit with them and ask, "What is the common theme between these? How can I turn these gifts, talents, and abilities into a financial feasibly profitable life?" You can make a living doing what you love and never work a day in your life when you 1) know what's important to you, 2) have clarity about what you do and don't like, and 3) know what you love doing.

"At the intersection where your gifts, talents, and abilities meet a human need; therein you will discover your purpose."
~ Aristotle

And, finally, now that you have clarified your true needs and desires and have a vision for your ideal job or career, take a few minutes to write a description of what your ideal job would look like in as much detail as possible. Where are you working? What are you doing? With whom are you working? What does a typical day look like? Is it your own business? Describe your customers or clients.

For example, you can start with:

My ideal job....

_____

_____

_____

_____

I encourage you to allow yourself to daydream, have fun with it, and make sure you get it on paper. Once you have it stated, put your attention on it. Reviewing it often will help keep you motivated and inspired. Think about it, talk about it, visualize it, and when you do, the right people, situations, and opportunities will begin to show up for you.

Dreams Do Come True!

I hope my story inspires you and I hope you can now see that your perfect job is looking for you, too!

Keep dreaming, stay open to all possibilities that seemingly come from out of the blue, because you never know... lots can happen!

Here's to YOUR Oh, My Gosh Moment.

OH, MY GOSH! NOW I KNOW WHAT I WANT TO DO WITH THE REST OF MY LIFE!

Jodi Santangelo-Ash

Jodi Santangelo-Ash is known as the Law of Attraction How-To Coach, teaching you how to apply the principles of the Law of Attraction to your life and business.

Drawing on her own personal life experiences and her love of training, she combines her Law of Attraction and Success Principles certifications to help people achieve their dreams and goals.

Through her years of speaking, training, and coaching, she has helped thousands of people across the country from all walks of life.

Jodi and her husband live in the historic town of St. Augustine, Florida.

When she's not training, she loves to ride on the back of her husband's Harley Davidson® motorcycle and traveling in their RV.

She is also the author of the book *Dynamic Affirmations* and creator of the program Reset, Refocus, Reengergize: 3 Simple Steps to Your Rapid Results.

Connect with Jodi at https://JodiSantangelo.com.

CHAPTER 9

Understanding Our Values to Find Joy

by Katie Evans

Whether we like it or not, whether we know it or not, all of our decisions are based on our values. As we navigate through life and, specifically through our careers, we constantly make choices that we believe will best serve our interests. To do this with intention, though, is how we bring joy to what we do.

In order to align ourselves with our values and use them as our guiding principles, we have to both identify and define what our values are. We need to do the self-reflection required to understand what matters most to us. We have to be vulnerable to do this.

My story

In my own experience, understanding my values changed everything about my career. In 2019, I was working at a great job. From all external views, I was doing really well. My job was a distinguished role, I was the youngest person in the history of the organization to hold that level of position, I worked with a wonderful staff, had a great boss, a short commute, and a generous salary and benefits package. Everything you could ever want, right? You'd think.

Somehow, despite all of these things, I found myself consistently unsatisfied. I grew restless and unhappy. Typically, I'm an obnoxious go-getter, but I could not seem to motivate myself. Even big, new projects weren't exciting to me.

As I recognized this unhappiness, I spiraled, and started to beat up myself for feeling this way. How could someone as fortunate as me feel unhappy? Why weren't all my great perks enough? What was wrong with me that I couldn't be grateful for what I had? I turned on myself, which did not help. I can assure you that the negative self-talk I began did not make me feel more satisfied with my career.

Fortunately, I have an incredible tribe of mentors who encouraged me to work with coaches to get to the bottom of this and figure out my next steps. I participated in some great courses and conversations, but the one that stuck out the most was where I participated in an activity to identify my values. That activity was facilitated by Dr. Janice Doucet Thompson who authored Chapter 2 of this book.

One of my values that really stuck out was "impact." As I define it, "impact" means that the work that I do has a positive effect on those I serve, the community is better because of the work I do, and that my team knows that they bring value to the community because they can see the difference their work makes to the people we serve.

The importance of impact helped me to see that while I was serving the community in my role, I was restricted to a particular customer base and my influence on that base was limited to the responsibilities of my particular role. Simply put, I felt that I had already done everything I was going to be able to do to make an impact in my community in my role.

Suddenly, as if the clouds had parted, I understood why I felt the way I did and how I could change it. The organization where I worked and the position that I had, while great, had very different priorities than I did. I was never going to be satisfied dedicating my life to work that was not aligned with the things that mattered most to me. And, most importantly, I didn't need to feel bad about it.

I was able to take immediate action. I reached out to my boss and explained what I was doing and he supported me. I started activating my network to let people know I was looking. I got serious about making a change.

I wrote my values and their definitions down in a place where I could reach them frequently. This was critical when I took action steps because it was easy to get off track. As an example, money was a low-priority value for me. So, when I started to look for jobs and received job offers with higher salaries than mine, it was easy to remind myself that money was not the important thing about a job.

Having my values handy was also important when people tried to talk me out of leaving my job. Friends, acquaintances, strangers, everyone, tried to tell me I was making a mistake. I'm sure they were doing this out of love and concern for me, but they all were wrong. I knew I was making the right choice, so when someone tried to warn me off, I could look at my values and know they did not understand.

Committing to my values led me to a job that I love, with a company I feel a very strong connection to, and my overall quality of life has increased.

Understanding your values

Consciously or unconsciously, values influence our feelings and our decisions. The best thing we can do for ourselves is to identify and define them.

While identifying values helped me to decide I wanted a new job, they can truly be used for anything. You can use your values to help determine what projects are most important to you and prioritize them. You can use them to help better manage your work/life balance. I once taught this activity to a colleague, who then went home and completed it with his wife to determine which preschool they wanted to send their child. You can be as specific as or general as you need to be.

A value is generally defined as something you find desirable, but I like to think of it as what's important to you. What matters in your day-to-day? What matters to you long-term?

It is critical to define our values individually. The same value word can have completely different meanings to different people. I'll go back to money as an example. A lot of people see wealth or money as a "greedy" value or one that's not very honorable. I have been privileged to generally live a comfortable life and money does not usually rise on my list. Conversely, I have a friend who has money in her top three because she wants to send two kids to college without loans, so that value means something different to her than it does to me. Another friend of mine grew up in poverty. Money, to her, means survival. It is her #1 value. Our perspectives matter a great deal.

Make this a zero-judgment activity for yourself. You do not need to explain why a value matters if you don't want to; it's more important to just know it matters. If you think people will judge you for your values, don't share them.

Values activity

If you are looking to feel joy about the work you do, I highly encourage you to participate in a values activity. There are a lot of ways to identify your values. You can find guided activities online. There are playing card sets that are fun to try. I've even done this in Excel using sorting and filter features. The important thing is that you use your own instincts and don't overthink the process.

Here is a simple way to figure out your values. Start with a long list of possible values. Here are some to get you started, but feel free to edit them:

* Achievement
* Affection
* Autonomy
* Beauty
* Challenge
* Communication
* Competence
* Competition
* Courage
* Creativity
* Curiosity
* Decisiveness
* Dependability
* Discipline
* Diversity
* Effectiveness
* Empathy
* Equality
* Faith

* Family
* Flexibility
* Freedom
* Friendship
* Growth
* Happiness
* Harmony
* Health
* Honesty
* Hope
* Humor
* Independence
* Innovation
* Integrity
* Intelligence
* Love
* Loyalty
* Open-mindedness
* Patience

* Power
* Productivity
* Prosperity
* Quality
* Recognition
* Respect
* Risk-taking
* Security
* Service
* Simplicity
* Spirituality
* Strength
* Success
* Teamwork
* Trust
* Truth
* Variety
* Wealth
* Wisdom

Put them on index cards, small pieces of paper, or sticky notes. Based on instinct alone, start flipping through them and sorting them into three piles: most important, important, least important. If you don't like those categories, you can change them to something you like better like red, yellow, green. Maybe instead of piles, you put them in your favorite hat, a hat you like, and a hat you have really been meaning to get rid of. Whatever works for you.

You need to do this sorting fast. Set a time for three minutes and hurry through it. Trust your gut.

When the timer goes off. Set the lowest priority pile aside. I mean it, don't flip through to see if there was something you really meant to put in another pile or just check to see if you want to rethink any. Set it aside. Get rid of it.

Mix your other two piles together again. Stand up. Walk around your office or kitchen or wherever you are. Take a deep breath.

Do it again. This time in two minutes.

Using only the values you've mixed together, make three piles without thinking and set aside the third pile. Again, step away for a moment to give yourself a break.

Then do it again. This time in one minute.

Hopefully by this time you are down to seven or eight values. If you are over ten, do the sorting portion of the activity again.

Now you can take some time to look at what you have. Maybe you are able to combine a few values. Or perhaps when you look at several you come up with another word that makes more sense and includes multiple values. Be thoughtful in this step and see if you can land on three to five values that really resonate with you.

Once you have settled on your values, it's time to define them. Take your time for this part. Think about what that value means to you. Why do you think you picked it? What are the impacts of that value? How does it apply to your daily life? How do you or could you work that value into your decisions?

As an example, here are a few of my current values (they change from time to time). They guide my actions.

- People
    - o Those around me know that they are appreciated and seen as individuals making important contributions.
    - o We can create change by assisting each other and working together.
- Impact
    - o The work that I do will have a positive impact on those that I serve.
    - o The community is better because of the work that I do.
    - o My team knows that they bring value to the community because they can see the difference that their work makes to the people we serve.
- Happiness
    - o Things that I do bring me joy.
    - o I am positive.
- Professional Development and Growth
    - o We all have the potential to be what we want to be.
    - o Learning is a lifelong commitment.

    o   I will support the efforts of others who want to learn.

- Innovation

    o   The way we've always done it may not be the right way.

    o   By taking risks, we discover new things.

Using your values

Create a document with your values and their definitions and refer to it as often as you need to. This can be a great resource as you grow and develop professionally or as you face other decisions.

If you're comfortable, share your values with those around you. I find that spouses are fascinated to learn about each other's. I once helped a colleague with this activity who thought his wife would be shocked by his results, but instead had selected almost the exact same values. This helped them open up communication about how their priorities had changed over time.

The group I was most eager to share my values with was the staff who reported to me. When they got to understand my values, it shifted our working relationship because of a new understanding between us and they had better insight into why I was asking for things. Though I had to be vulnerable to share, and it was hard, it provided a genuine bond amongst our group.

I want to warn you that your values will change over time. Please be prepared for that and be willing to pivot when you need to. Repeat this activity as often as you need to, but try to do it every few years.

This type of self-reflection allows us to bring joy to what we do by better aligning ourselves with our ideals. Understanding what we want to contribute to the world and how we want to engage with it provides guidance that can set us on a path to meaningful and fulfilling work.

Katie Evans

Katie Evans is Senior Communications Strategist for Woodard & Curran where she assists clients with public facing outreach, strategic communications, and engagement facilitation. Katie has experience with stakeholder engagement and outreach, relationship development, crisis communication, and communication strategy building. She has worked extensively on Disadvantaged Community water-related issues.

Katie holds a bachelor's degree in Journalism and Mass Communications from Arizona State University, and a master's degree in Public Policy Administration from Northwestern University. She has served in various communications and water management positions in public agencies and including Director of Communications and Conservation for Coachella Valley Water District.

Katie has served on a variety of committees for the Association of California Water Agencies and participates with the Arizona Water Association, California Association of Public Information Officers, American Water Works Association, and National Water Resources Association. Katie is the immediate past steering committee chair of the California Data Collaborative. She is a graduate of the Leadership California - California Issues and Trends program.

Katie is originally from the Coachella Valley in Southern California, but currently lives in Phoenix, Arizona.

Connect with Katie at https://www.linkedin.com/in/katieevanswc.

————◆◆◆————

CHAPTER 10

Finding Joy in Work: It's an Inside Job

by Keri White, SHRM-SCP

Let's face it, most of us spend years doing a job that may not be what we truly want to do. Now more than ever, people want to experience more meaningful work. What about you? Do you sit at your desk daily wishing you could be or do something else? Do you feel stifled or stuck in your career? Do you daydream about your purpose, or maybe you know your purpose, but you feel as though you could never earn enough money doing that purposeful work?

If any of these scenarios sound familiar, you are not alone. According to Pew Research Center, only 49% of Americans are fully satisfied with their jobs.[1] That means one in every two people is unsatisfied or fulfilled with their daily work. Consider how many hours you work each week. Now, imagine how much more joy you would experience if you were fulfilled by what you did. It is time to re-evaluate your work.

While the recent global pandemic negatively impacted many people, others got to reset, pivot, reevaluate priorities, and rest. Many people also experienced job layoffs during this time, which forced a reevaluation of work. Moreover, in August 2021, more than 4.3 million people quit their jobs, according to The Harvard Gazette.[2] This exodus from the job market has been appropriately coined as "Great Resignation." People quit during that time for several reasons, but many quit to pursue entrepreneurship, education, or new careers. Despite the uncertainty of the pandemic, people chose to embark on a new path.

They took back their power to choose the life they wanted to lead, and their actions and decisions aligned with that mindset. What is stopping you from shifting your life today? There is so much joy in doing the work you want to be doing. That joy is not about a paycheck. It is about the intrinsic satisfaction of choosing the path that gives you greater fulfillment.

Journal Prompt: What is keeping you from doing the work you love?

Despite what you may have written in your journal, here is some tough love needed to help you go deeper with your answers to this question. Y-O-U are the only thing keeping you from work you love. Ownership and accountability are critical if you want to shift into truly loving the work you perform. Blaming your circumstances, boss, coworkers, spouse, children, or any other person or thing negates the fact that you have the power to shift your reality. No matter how old you are, how many children you have, how much money you have, or where you live, you can change your life. Don't believe it? Then, keep reading.

To change your life, there are a few things you will need to do first, and they are all an inside job. Doing these things will help you shift from a position of weakness to a position of power. You will shift from thinking you can't to knowing you can! That's right! You can change your life and that change can start today. You decide.

Ultimately, finding joy in your work is an inside job. Yes, you must shift your inner self-talk to change your reality. Speaking powerful mantras daily will help you shift in every area of your life, including work.

Journal Prompt: What are your interests, values, and strengths? What are the aspects of work where you thrive? What have you always envisioned doing for work?

Speaking powerful mantras daily is a simple solution, but it is not necessarily easy to do, because limiting beliefs rob so many of reaching true success. Do you truly know that you deserve success and that you can achieve your definition of success? It is important that you know you deserve and can obtain success, because it is easy to begin feeling like a fraud or an impostor along your path to success. Yes! Impostor syndrome is a real psychological issue many high achievers experience at some point in their careers.

How many times have you thought, who am I to deserve this status or achievement? What makes me the expert? What if people don't support me because they know my past? The list of doubts can go on and on if allowed. That's the key – if we allow it!

This is where an important decision must be made. This one decision can determine success or failure. This one decision can also determine your physical, emotional, and mental well-being or lack thereof. This decision can determine whether you have the career and life of your dreams.

Here's the question you must ask yourself: Will I let my doubts overpower me, or will I overpower my doubts?

While this is a simple question, overcoming doubts and impostor syndrome is not easy. When I got my first executive leadership role. I was the youngest on the team with the least amount of experience. I was the only Black person and one of only two women on the team. Talk about intimidating!

On the one hand, I could have congratulated myself for having earned this position on the corporate ladder. Instead, I often questioned whether I deserved my role. This completely undermined my years of experience, degrees, certifications, skill set, and results. I would sit in boardrooms around the ominous wooden tables and discuss corporate strategy, profit and loss statements, and organizational development with top leaders. Yet, in the back of my mind, I felt like an impostor.

Sounds crazy, right? Trust me, impostor syndrome can happen to the best of us. Although common sense would tell me I was right where I belonged, negative thoughts would take over and fester. For me to enjoy my work and be effective, I knew I had to change my stinkin' thinking! Because impostor syndrome is often connected to our mental messages, the simplest, most effective method to overcome it is to create mantras to shift our mindset. After all, we are what we think!

Once I incorporated powerful mantras into my daily routine, I could lead from a place of confidence and power while maintaining compassion for others. How awesome would it be for you to shift from feeling like an impostor to feeling like a powerful, confident person ready to shift into the work you enjoy?

While I know it's not easy to make this mental shift, I also know it's 100% doable. How do I know? I know because I did the work and made it happen for myself. I shifted from feeling unworthy and unconfident to owning my worth and value while powerfully and confidently leading in the marketplace.

So, you may be wondering what I did exactly. It's simple. I made a mindset shift by creating and reciting powerful mantras. I repeated these powerful mantras every time a negative thought entered my mind. These mantras were designed to strategically combat every negative thought that limited my ability to lead confidently and excellently. They helped me overcome fears and allowed me to choose the path that felt most right to me. Because the words we repeat in our thought-life are vital to what we experience in our real life, I had to create mantras that eradicated the negative and replaced them with action-focused, powerfully positive new thoughts.

Below are a couple of examples of mantras I created to shift from stinkin' thinkin' to powerful thinking:

Stinkin' Thinking Mantra: I don't deserve to be in the room with these more experienced people because I am new to this field.

Powerful Mantra: I have earned my role and deserve to be in the room. My results, experience, education, and skills got me here, and they will take me to the next level.

Stinkin' Thinking Mantra: I am too old to change careers now.

Powerful Mantra: I have done hard things before and can do this now. I will change my career and find joy in my work life.

Do you see the shift in language between the Stinkin' Thinking Mantras and the Powerful Mantras? Do you see how the shift in language can change your mindset, posture, self-esteem, and your reality?

This is precisely what you need to do to change your life! Explore your negative self-talk. Determine how impostor syndrome may have infected your mind. Then, create action-focused, powerful mantras that eradicate negativity and create space for you in the marketplace to find joy in your work.

It is important to eradicate the bad habit of stinkin' thinking. To think you don't deserve success or that you are not worthy of the life you desire limits your life immeasurably. It minimizes your ability to conquer your goals and find joy in your life and in your work. It diminishes your value in the marketplace. It smothers your dreams. Also, stinkin' thinking is infectious. It spreads like wildfire, negatively impacting others, which is not the impact you want to make.

Occasionally, I wonder where I would be if I had decided to let impostor syndrome overpower me. I wouldn't have the career I love, nor would I have impacted so many lives. I would not enjoy abundance and my children would not have a real-life example of what it means to set goals, achieve them, and then help others achieve their goals and dreams. Honestly, the tentacles of overcoming stinkin' thinking are far-reaching.

Every day I am grateful I made the powerful decision to overcome stinkin' thinking and find joy in my work because I get to authentically lead from a place of confidence, power, and excellence. Ridding yourself of all thoughts that don't align with your goals and dreams will free you to excel in ways you can't yet imagine. You will touch lives you never knew you could. You will rise up the ladder of success. The impact you will create once your mind shifts from stinkin' thinking to powerful thinking is immeasurable.

Joy in your work is available for all who choose to make the shift in your mindset. Own the fact that you get to decide whether you are overpowered by stinkin' thinking or whether you overpower stinkin' thinking. Know that the decision is yours alone.

The bottom line is, it does not matter who supports you and who does not. It does not matter at all what others think of you. Truly, what you think and believe about yourself is the only thing that matters. You have the power within you to shift your thinking to align with the great life you desire! It's all up to you. Choose wisely. You're worth it!

1. How Americans View Their Jobs | Pew Research Center March 30, 2023

2. Harvard economist sheds light on 'Great Resignation' – Harvard Gazette October 20, 2021

Keri White

Keri White is CEO of BeeBetter HR, LLC and Wealthy Futures, LLC. Keri is an accomplished business coach, award-winning speaker, and best-selling author. She has over 20 years of experience improving businesses' performance, leading successful teams, and generating revenue. With a proven track record of leading and transforming organizations, Keri has earned a reputation for her strategic vision, business acumen, and ability to drive results.

As a coach, Keri uniquely inspires and empowers others to unlock their inner greatness. Through her coaching practice, she has guided individuals in identifying their goals, overcoming obstacles, and taking meaningful action toward success. Keri's coaching style is characterized by her empathy and gift for helping her clients achieve results.

Keri is also a best-selling author and award-winning speaker who captivates audiences with engaging and empowering messages. Known for her ability to connect deeply with people, Keri delivers powerful messages that motivate and ignite positive change.

Keri's energy and passion are contagious, leaving a lasting impact on everyone.

Also, Keri contributes to her community by mentoring aspiring leaders and volunteering her time and expertise to various nonprofit organizations. Whether through her businesses or service, Keri's passion for making a positive impact is evident in everything she does as she inspires and empowers others to realize their full potential.

Connect with Keri at www.beebetterhr.com.

CHAPTER 11

———————•❀•———————

Spread Love: It's the Brooklyn Way

by Khalil Anthony Sikander Jr.

I work in one of the most dynamic professions where you can express your love for your content and for the human race through the love of what I do. As an Educator, Coach and Educational Speaker, I have experiences daily that show me why the world is a significant place. With two decades of experience as a physical education instructor and coach, I have learned so much about myself, our youth, and educators. I have come to know what most youths and adults want. Love. When I now visit a classroom, speak at an assembly or teacher conference as a speaker and have people visit with me after my message and say "I needed this message today," or "I'm extremely thankful for your stories and what you taught me," my heart is filled with a spiritual juice that tastes like the best piña colada I have ever had. In that moment, I am there with those individuals giving and receiving love of why I love what I do.

It's ironic, but I learned to love what I do through love. This love was ingrained in me the first 21 years of my life growing up in my hometown of Brooklyn, New York. Our perspective comes from experiences, whether good or bad. Some people see New Yorkers as blunt, hard-nosed, and rude people. What I see is truth, honesty, and meaningful expressions of the heart. There is love in those expressions, though many may not see it. The skill of love is taught and learned through these expressions. I was taught not to hide my faults and that love is behind it. It's something I admire about where I'm from and I'm thankful for it.

I was blessed as a youngster to soak in the sea of diverse cultures in the concrete jungle unlike anywhere in the world. This chapter title, "Spread Love It's The Brooklyn Way," is fitting because so much love is there. These spoken words are lyrics by the legendary iconic rapper, Notorious B.I.G., and they ring true. With so many people coming from different places, it's a necessary part of life to learn about others. Understanding another person's culture is the start of how we love that allows us to become closer to each other. I was blessed that my best friend was African-American and that my neighborhood friends were of the Puerto Rican and Dominican background. It gave me insight into our cultural differences to help me grow as a person. Being of Afghani descent, I felt lost at times because I was alone. I didn't connect to other cultures as I was the minority in my neighborhood. With being a basketball enthusiast, I learned so much about myself because I was celebrated by others for my love of the game. I was embraced by the African-American community who played this sport nonstop. I learned to talk, act, and feel a part of this community. Brooklyn was the ideal place for learning to love what I do.

Without the positive influences by my mentors and teachers, there is no telling what I would become. When they say it takes an army to raise a child, it was absolutely true in my case. My home was plagued with alcoholism and abuse. I didn't grow up with my biological dad.

I didn't have the father and son relationship I wanted. I rarely heard the words, "I love you." I knew my mom loved me, but circumstances made it hard for me to feel her love the way I needed to feel it. When I stepped outside of my 3-story apartment, I passed the bodega on the street corner where many of my friends or family were selling drugs. I entered my neighborhood park to play basketball, but made sure to watch my surroundings so I wasn't around when the violence erupted. That love I talked about earlier showed up in many situations, such as when those who were involved in sticky situations told me to leave so I could be safe if something bad happened. Without the influence of those who saw good in me, I couldn't have the influence I have today. Those experiences created the man I am.

As a kid, I searched for love either in the wrong crowd roaming the streets or on the blacktop courts. Love was rare at home. These were the two options I knew about. There were more, but I didn't know how to explore them. I was lucky to love basketball and grasped the game easily. It was at the age of 13 that I had a defining moment that changed my life forever. I was playing in a basketball tournament and I did the unthinkable, something I would never live down, something you would never think. I actually shot the ball into the wrong basket (yeah, I did that). After a subway train ride of embarrassment with friends, due to that infamous shot, I promised myself to never feel that way again.

After five years of being cared for by two amazing coaches who were my father figures, I built a strong work ethic that changed my life. It wasn't easy. I battled my personal spiritual demons to avoid using drugs and alcohol. With daily encounters with illegal substances that were easily accessible no matter where I turned, eventually I fell victim. Relentlessly, I stood in this spiritual boxing ring with my opponents of my inner doubt and the pressure of my poverty-stricken surroundings. These doubts would tell me that this negative life was meant for me. I went round for round with this curse. The curse of being another person who had potential to leave this destruction and change his life for the better, but got entangled by these chains of despair. This constant thought and burden were on my soul. Daily I would have to put on my inner soul boxing gloves to defeat these opponents so I could become the best basketball player I could be. Through my dedication, I ascended to becoming a top player in New York City. The love of the game led me to leave New York City to chase my dream of playing division one basketball. Due to my academic failures and poor life choices, the journey was long and treacherous because I landed myself at Colorado Northwestern Community College in Rangely, Colorado, and started my junior college career in a town with one streetlight. Talk about culture shock. I left the Big Apple for the desert oil fields in western Colorado. From there, I made my way down to Southern Utah University, a small division one school in Cedar City, Utah (a hop, skip, and a jump away from the infamous Zion National Park), where I received my bachelor's degree, later finished my Master's Degree, and accomplished my dream. I was able to do and see things I only saw on TV when I was a kid. I look back now and wish I could rewrite some of my choices as I know the path would have been different. Regardless, the game provided great memories and experiences that I do not take for granted.

I was fortunate for the great mentors and teachers in my life that helped me down this path. I look back now to see why I love what I do and what B.I.G.'s lyrics really mean to me. Their love for me opened my eyes to opportunities to change my life. I learned that love was more than receiving hugs and kisses and hearing the words "I love you." Their influence is why I followed in their footsteps. Their imprint of faith on me has to be continued and that is why I do what I do.

As an educator, loving what you do is communicated in many ways. I love what I do because my profession frequently provides these opportunities.

When we come into this world, we are given the right to be valued, honored, and esteemed. That should never stop. As adults and leaders, we oftentimes forget that all we want as humans is to be loved. When you don't feel that in your work life or home life, it makes living very difficult.

Through my experiences, I have learned that to love my job is not in "what I do" that makes a difference, but in "how I do it." My mentors taught me this as a youngster. Our "how" is where we lead ourselves to receiving and giving these hugs especially in a school setting. Let me explain.

We can all remember a teacher, coach, or mentor who made a positive impact in our lives. What did they do for you? These individuals most likely gave you a feeling of worth. They saw you, they heard you, and they cared for you. Many life lessons were taught and learned. And those lessons stick with you to this day. You probably can think of a moment right now. Pause for a moment. Reflect on that individual. Can you find the love in that story? I bet you can.

You see, the love they shared was through their spirit. They shared the gift of who they truly were and you received it. The love shown was through having tough conversations that gave solutions to problems in a productive manner so you could become a better person. The love shown made a connection on a human level. The love they shared was through their personal culture that allowed them to find joy and transcend it to you. You learned from a deeper place because of it. They exemplified love through truth and confrontation. Just like a blunt New Yorker sometimes does. This gave you the ability to truly be yourself.

Loving what you do gives an experience that pierces the soul and leaves a positive scar on your heart that reminds you that love inspires improvement. These educators made the world a better place for you. There isn't a person on earth who truly has been successful without feeling loved or giving love to others. Our youth wants love, the education world wants love, and the business world wants love. I've been blessed that this gift has been given to me and I have accepted it. This brings me joy as I get to do this as my mentors did for me.

Knowing your value and knowing your worth allows your heart to find its true purpose. One of my greatest joys is having the gift of guiding people to rise through the ashes to become the phoenix they were meant to be. The fact is, we all are educators no matter our field and are capable of doing this in any profession. As you look back on your educational experience, you became a phoenix many times when certain teachers touched your life. A still, small voice inside you revealed itself. Every time we feel loved, we find this voice. This voice continues to tell you how important you are to this earth. Love unleashes your greatness. Being gifted the ability to help people find their greatness creates absolute bliss in my life.

I am blessed to love the gifts I receive every day of helping others change their future. I get to help people transform by speaking from a place that allows for connection that doesn't come from this universe. Every day my spiritual connections to my duty as a human to be authentically real guides someone closer to becoming the next greatest athlete, teacher, entrepreneur, or scientist the world needs. It's true. I have been blessed to see some of my former athletes reach their dreams of playing in the NFL, professional basketball players overseas, successful engineers, doctors, and entrepreneurs. I have been fortunate enough to have a former student athlete name their child after me. Wow, what a Blessing! I've seen the other side where kids have overcome cancer, parental divorce, a friend's death by suicide, and so much more. I have also faced my own challenges as a teacher facing racial discrimination, bullying, harassment, and almost losing my educational career due to hate while watching my students experience their own challenges. When we love through challenging times, we create and build strong people who can deal with the worst that humanity has to offer. Knowing that I help others find their worth by my positive influence while either experiencing positive or tough times is a fulfilling reward.

Loving what you do shines your joy. It illuminates an aura about you. Many will want to know about that light. Our identities don't come from what we do, but who we are. That is that light. This is the true way we love what we do. Love builds strong and unstoppable humans. The ultimate goal is to learn that success is bigger than yourself. Honestly, I believe this is how you can do the impossible. I've seen it and lived it. Your love for yourself and others gives you limitless opportunities to touch the stars. I love what I do because what I do on a daily basis changes lives forever, including my own.

Khalil Anthony Sikander Jr.

Being diagnosed with post-traumatic stress disorder (PTSD) due to childhood and adult traumas, which include racism, abuse, alcoholism, and the death of loved ones, Khalil Anthony Sikander Jr. knows all about pain. Khalil has battled this demon and searched for an answer in all of his traumatizing experiences. The conclusion: "Love."

His inspiration came from the song "Juicy" by the great Notorious B.I.G. "Spread Love it's the Brooklyn Way" were the lyrics that replayed in his mind while reflecting on his childhood growing up in Brooklyn enduring his darkest moment in life. Khalil, an educator, former teacher, and coach of the year turned speaker and author, speaks on how acts of love saved his life and how we can do the same for others.

Connect with Khalil at www.cultureofluv.com.

CHAPTER 12

The Joy of an Amazing Network

by Leah Hoyer

I make video games for a living. That may sound like a ton of fun, and some days it is. It is also complex, highly political, and still heavily male dominated. It can also be quite unstable. Projects are frequently cancelled, studios close, and people can find themselves out of a job with little warning. That has happened to quite a few game developers recently, as companies around the globe are looking for places to cut expenses. This year, that's just what happened to me and my team.

In late 2020, I was recruited by Wizards of the Coast, makers of Dungeons & Dragons and Magic: The Gathering, to start a new video game studio within the company. Our mission was to create a brand-new franchise for the company, one that would reach a younger, broader demographic than their existing properties. Things were going very well. We had a great story world, appealing art style, and innovative gameplay that had all tested well with potential customers. We grew our team with more excellent people, had a strong studio culture, and were ahead of schedule and under budget. We were crushing it!

The economy, however, was not doing so well. In late 2022, budgets were tightened and the company made the tough decision to cut projects that didn't support their existing franchises. That included our project. It was an understandable business decision, but our team was crushed. We loved our game, we loved our team, and we knew something special was about to die because of bad timing. As the head of the studio, I was most concerned about the people who were about to lose their jobs. Not only were they great at what they did, they were also amazing teammates and people.

This showed over the next couple of weeks as we went into the end-of-year holiday break knowing that we were going to be laid off in the next couple of months. The way this team rallied around each other by sharing job leads, offering to make introductions, and just generally reaching out to make sure their teammates were okay reminded all of us that we weren't doing this alone and that people still had our backs. The months or years we had worked together created a true bond, not just a business relationship.

When I returned to the office in the new year, I had a new plan, largely inspired by the passion and loyalty this group showed to each other and the project. While the company we were working for might not be able to keep the project going, maybe we could? I've spent my career developing new entertainment properties. One huge lesson I've taken away from that is that the projects that are going to be a hit are just easier to make. Not easy. Making a video game or TV series is never easy, but they flow. The vision makes sense and the team rallies around it, making the project smoother. This project was one of the smoothest I'd ever been involved with. That is so rare, and it seemed worth my time to see if we could keep it rolling on our own.

So this year, I've become an entrepreneur. I struck a deal with Wizards to bring the project to my own company, Level Headed Games.

The best part is that several of those former teammates are on board as well. I know we can make an amazing game and build a truly excellent company. I also know that it is going to be a lot of work.

Frankly, it already has been. While our small crew makes progress on building our game, my focus has been building the company that can support those efforts. From purchasing computers and software licenses, to establishing partnerships that can help with our production pipelines, to dusting off the social media accounts that I had let go dormant the past couple of years, the ridiculously varied checklist of tasks that has become my job description these past few months is daunting. Thankfully, I'm not tackling it alone.

These past several months have shown me that, over the course of my life, I have cultivated an amazing network of people.

When I started telling people that I was building a new games studio, there were certainly a good number of comments about how hard that was going to be. However, looking back on these past several months, I'm struck by the fact that not one person told me it was a bad idea or tried to talk me out of it. Instead, the comments included things like, "Of course you are," "I would work at your company," and one very exuberant, "I love this for you!" More often than not, the words of encouragement would be followed by, "How can I help?"

I value this network highly, and for many reasons. Some of these people are high powered and influential. They've fired off introductions and recommendations to other key players in the games industry, helping to expand my circle of contacts in a matter of minutes. What I have been continually impressed by, though, is the time these terribly busy people have spent with me to share lessons they've learned about corporate board formation, review my pitch deck with a critical eye, or explain the finer points of a SAFE note. They could easily charge thousands of dollars for these services, but they've made themselves available to me, sometimes without me even having to ask.

Most of my network, however, fill more modest roles. Some I have known since grade school, a couple I am related to, many I met at work-related conferences, one I met at Women's Rock Camp, and the vast majority were former colleagues I met at work. Their offers to help have been just as inspiring. The fact that a good number of our teammates were interested in staying together as part of this new venture is particularly affirming. Then there are those folks who have surprised me as they stepped forward, saying things like, "We didn't work very closely together, but I always enjoyed the times we did. Let me know if I can be of help in any way." Those actions are humbling, and remind me that real connections are formed when you have true curiosity about others and treat them with respect.

Of all my accomplishments in my career, the creation of this network is what I am most proud of. It is evidence that I've formed true connections with people. Many business relationships are superficial and temporary, formed at a time when you could each do something to benefit the other. I'm sure many of my LinkedIn connections fall into this category. Those relationships aren't bad, they are just thin. My true network is eagerly, proactively asking how they can help, knowing that right now, I have little to offer in return.

I am in awe of the generosity of my true network. They have been and will continue to be a huge part of my successes. Through the ups and downs of starting a company, this incredible network propels me forward and is a consistent source of joy.

Leah Hoyer

Leah Hoyer is the founder and CEO of Level Headed Games, where she and the team are setting a new bar for cooperative online video games. Prior to her new venture, Ms. Hoyer was GM and Vice President of Creative for Wizards of the Coast's New IP Studio. She has developed and produced television series, video games, and interactive experiences for some of the world's most beloved entertainment companies (Disney, Xbox, Telltale Games, Bungie) for over twenty years. She is a recognized expert in interactive storytelling and franchise development across various media. She is passionate about supporting diverse voices in entertainment and working to make everyone feel that gaming is for them.

Connect with Leah at https://levelheadedgames.com/.

CHAPTER 13

49 Jobs in 36 Years

by Lynda Sunshine West

Yep, I had 49 jobs in 36 years.

The joy of work? Anyone who has had that number of jobs, obviously, does not enjoy work. So why am I writing a chapter in this book? Read on and you'll see.

Oh, by the way, I never got fired from a single job. I quit all of my jobs except one job where they laid off 500 people and I was one of the 500.

I started working at age 16 at a local county fair in San Diego, California. I was a cotton candy maker. That was a fun job and it enabled me to buy some rainbow shirts, Dove shorts, and red Reebok high-top shoes (my favorite shoes ever). Those brands were all the rage back in the late 1970s. I thought I was cool because I wore designer clothes. My job and making my own money gave me this gift.

One of my few fond memories of my dad is when we were at the fair. I went to buy cotton candy from one of the merchants whose shop was set up in a food truck. I saw a Help Wanted sign and asked about the job. They interviewed me on the spot and I was hired. I guess they were so desperate to hire someone, anyone who was breathing, because I had zero experience.

I was so excited and went to tell my dad that I got a job.

He said, "How are you going to get here?"

I said, "I didn't think about that."

This is a prime example of going after what you want and not worrying about the "how." I didn't know it at the time, but I was practicing manifestation.

All I knew was that I got the job and I was going to be able to afford to buy my own clothes for the first time in my life. I was going to be free of relying on my mom and dad and I could buy what I wanted when I had the money. My own money was going to enable me to live the life I want to live. Money was going to make a huge difference in my life. That's all I knew.

You see, I grew up in a very volatile, abusive alcoholic household with four siblings (I was kid #4) and we kids were better seen than heard. I ran away when I was five years old and was gone an entire week. I only went to the neighbor's house, so I was safe. Something happened during that week when I was gone. Nobody came to get me. At age five, because no one came to get me, I had a belief that became locked tight into my brain and that was that nobody came to get me because they don't love me and they don't want me around. When my mom brought me home after the week was done, I became a people pleaser and became riddled with fears.

So, at age 16 (11 years later) when my dad asked me how I was going to get to my job, I didn't know how to respond because I was filled with fear and thought he would be mad at me.

His response, though, surprised me. He said, "Well, I guess we need to get your driver's license tomorrow." I'm embarrassed to admit that I was overjoyed that I was going to get my driver's license, but that kind act of his went unnoticed. For me, his volatility overshadowed any kindness he had.

Here I am 44 years later and I finally recognize all the good things my dad did for me and have gratitude for his actions. Unfortunately, I didn't come around until many years after he passed away. This isn't the story about my dad, so I'll continue with my work journey.

The next morning we got up and dad took me to the Department of Motor Vehicles to get my license. I took my driving test and passed with flying colors. I was more free than I had ever been in my life. I was now a California driver. I could go wherever I wanted. I could even drive myself to work.

There was only one hitch. I didn't have a car.

My dad, however, gave me the keys to the car and let me drive to work by myself, 30 miles from our house.

That five weeks of working at the fair was the first door that was opened for me in my work "career." After the fair was over, I had a taste of what it was like to make my own money.

My next job was working at a local fast food restaurant. (Don't worry, I'm not going to take you through all 49 of my jobs.) I worked at that job and excelled. I became the trainer at that restaurant and that set in motion my ability to train people at every job I had. I was able to catch on to the tasks at hand quickly and, therefore, was a valuable employee and my employers saw that in me and used my skills to their greatest capacity.

As happened at just about every job I ever had, though, I ended up getting bored and felt unappreciated. I showed up to work early every day, rarely took a lunch break or snack break, and oftentimes would leave late. All of my reviews were stellar, and I was very well-liked. (Not everybody liked me, but most did.)

I remember this one woman who called me a brown noser. She was in her 40s and I was 20. I was working as a bank teller at a local credit union and she had it in for me. She used to talk about me behind my back (loud enough that I could hear her) to some of our customers and my co-workers and that pissed me off, but I was too scared to say something to her because she was scary and intimidating. I had never met anyone like her before.

She was poorly behaved for about six months until one day when I simply lost it. I flipped my lid. The lunchroom was right next to where the teller station was. She was in the lunchroom talking to another co-worker. I heard the older woman mention my name and say how I'm a brown noser and that I would do anything I had to do in order to get ahead. This was totally false. I showed up every day and did my work and helped others to do their work if they needed help. I was the furthest thing from being a brown noser. I was just a hard worker and took pride in my work. She was a lazy worker and saw me as a threat, so she would talk about me behind my back.

Something was different that day, though. I was like a caged animal that had been unlocked from the cage and I was no longer going to take it. I was fed up. I ran into the lunchroom and screamed at her in a whisper (I didn't want the customers to hear me). I called her the F word and the B word. (Those are words I don't normally say, so for me to say them out loud to somebody was way out of my character.) She just sat there staring at me in shock. I was shocked, too. I had never in my entire life ever done anything like that.

As I shared earlier, when I came home at five years old, I became riddled with fear. One of my greatest fears was that people wouldn't like me and the fear of judgment. By me yelling at her in a whisper, I risked the fear of judgment and the fear of her not liking me. Realistically, she didn't like me anyway, so what was I afraid of? Even though she didn't like me, I still wanted her to like me. I had this deep desire to be liked by everybody. I now know how foolish that was, but at that time in my life, it was what I desperately wanted and needed. I think it's because I felt rejected when I was five years old and nobody came to get me.

When I walked out of the lunchroom, there was a line of customers waiting to be helped at the teller window. Many of them were applauding me as I walked out of the lunchroom. It was a silent applause with their hands in front of their bodies in a slow and silent clap. That was when I realized that the customers knew what was going on. I was embarrassed that I had spoken to my elder in that way, but I was no longer going to be treated in that way by her.

I ended up becoming a teller supervisor at that credit union and quit after 1 1/2 years. I loved being a bank teller and supervisor, but I was a salaried employee and was working 70 to 80 hours a week and making less than $3 an hour. Minimum wage at that time was $3.10 an hour, so I was making less than minimum wage as a supervisor. Every time I asked my boss to lower my hours, she would lower them for about a week and then they would creep right back up to 70 to 80 hours a week. I had two babies at home and never saw them.

After I quit that job, I was searching for a job where I would make a good amount of money and be appreciated. After 36 years in the workforce and 49 jobs, I can honestly say that I never found what I was looking for.

I had made my way up the ladder and was working for a judge in the 9th Circuit Court of Appeals. I worked there for 13 months and had a huge epiphany that I hated my job, yet again. It was a boring job where I called myself a glorified travel agent. I had amazing federal government benefits and was making close to six figures, but was thoroughly bored.

In November 2014, at age 51, I decided to leave the corporate world and become an entrepreneur. I work more than 70 or 80 hours a week now and I can't imagine doing anything other than what I do.

I spent the first six years as an entrepreneur trying to figure out what I love doing, who I want to serve, how I will serve them, and how to make money doing it. I have invested a lot of money and time into my business. I always had this feeling that there was more for me to do in the world, it was just not going to be at a job where I was working for somebody else who doesn't appreciate what I have to offer.

Just like my corporate life, I have tried a lot of things as an entrepreneur. There were several times that I wanted to throw in the towel and just give up on myself because it didn't seem as if I was ever going to be successful. But the idea of going back to a job was so much worse than my failing as an entrepreneur. I'm so glad I stuck it out because as the publisher of this book that you are reading, this journey has been so worth it. I've had so many ups and downs, twists and turns, fronts and backs and sideways, and one thing has held true the whole time: my desire for something better.

In business, we are often asked, "What is your why? Why do you do what you do?"

Why am I a book publisher?

The answer is simple for me. When I started sharing my story in my book, The Year of Fears, it not only transformed my own mind, but also transformed the life of people who have read my book. I know the power of our stories. I know the value of putting our messages into the world. I also know how scary it can be to share your story.

In 2015, I broke through one fear every single day for an entire year, hence The Year of Fears. Breaking through those fears has given me an advantage as a book publisher because I am able to help my clients break through their fears of sharing their own stories. I totally get it and there's no judgment when working with me. I have helped hundreds of people get their message into the world to make a greater impact on the planet.

It took me several decades to get to this place in my life and I'm so glad I was persistent and stuck it out. There is no greater joy than living the life you truly want to live.

Lynda Sunshine West

She ran away at 5 years old and was gone an entire week, came home riddled with fears and, in turn, became a people-pleaser. At age 51, she decided to break through one fear every day for a year and, in doing so, she gained an exorbitant amount of confidence to share her story. Her mission is to empower 5 million women and men to write their stories to make a greater impact on the planet. Lynda Sunshine West is the Founder and CEO of Action Takers Publishing, a Speaker, 25 Time #1 International Bestselling Author, Contributing Writer at Entrepreneur Magazine and Brainz Magazine, Executive Film Producer, and Red Carpet Interviewer.

Connect with Lynda Sunshine at www.actiontakerspublishing.com.

CHAPTER 14

The Ride of a Lifetime

by Nicole Townsend

I turned fifty in 2022. The half-century milestone. It was a moment to look back on my life and what I'd accomplished so far. Part of that, of course, was reflecting on my career. I realized that my life's work has always centered around people and their experiences. My interest led me to cultivate my childhood curiosity in people's stories, unveiled a passion for developing great company leaders, and enabled me to start a company focused on employee experience. As I look back on my career, I realize it has been one great ride—exhilarating at some points and terrifying at others—with each twist preparing me for the next turn.

What I've learned from my own experiences is that finding fulfillment through work is somewhat of an emotional roller coaster. There are ups and downs that make us scream in exhilaration and cry out in fear. There are twists and turns that jerk us around and lift us off our seats. And, without experiencing this ride marked with wins and losses, we would not know the strength, resilience and commitment it took to get on it in the first place. We would not know the journey that got us to stand in line and wait was, perhaps, preparing us for the adventure to come.

I was raised by two hardworking parents from an era more likely to seek stability than fulfillment in work. A job could become a career—but a job was really meant to help people support their families. My dad's mantra of life priorities was "Family. Work. Home." He repeated it throughout my life. My mom liked to remind us, "There is no fun until the work is done," which meant, "Finish your chores before heading to the mall." There was no such thing as resting on a weekend—at least until Sunday evening. Then, we rested to prepare for the week ahead. It was an ongoing loop.

It's no wonder that I started working at a young age. When I was 11, I was a mother's helper for my mom's best friend who had sweet twin babies and an "active" toddler. I rode shotgun in her silver Volvo as we lugged the kids to appointments and on errands, listening to cool music. As an industrious 13-year-old babysitter, I racked up gigs on Fridays and Saturdays in my neighborhood. Not only babysitting, but cooking and cleaning, I had five-star ratings and rave reviews before Yelp. I moved on to my first part-time job at age fifteen at a local farmer's market and auction where I slung hot dogs and polish sausages at an orange and yellow cart in the 100-degree heat. I wore my branded uniform and change dispenser belt with pride and sunburn on my face.

I was moving up after graduating high school and landed a job at a local, family-owned grocery chain. I chose to work at the store a bit further from my house so I could experience life in another area of town. I liked the old store, built and opened the year I was born, more than the brand-new store in my neighborhood. It was like its own world, with people of all ages, from all over town working together. It was hard work, yet we made it fun, and we made it matter. We connected with our customers. We would play, "Name that Total," with some regulars, encouraging them to guess the grand total as I bagged their groceries. We connected with each other. We challenged ourselves to bring in as many carts as our arms could steer without smashing our fingers. It was the first time I worked on a real team. *I loved the connection.*

All the while, I was attending college, majoring in journalism. My long-time goal was to become a newspaper reporter. In junior high, I had set my sights on becoming a modern Lois Lane. After college and an internship, I landed my "dream job" at a community newspaper that was part of the city's main paper. I chose the roughest, toughest beat in town—to my parent's chagrin. "You're always walking on the edge of danger," my mom said, with a shake of her head. I couldn't help it. It was exhilarating to me.

It is where I learned the most about people—by spending time with them, enveloping all my senses in the moment and telling their stories. There I was, my long, blond braid spilling out of a black beret, wearing baggy jeans and black Doc Marten boots in search of stories that needed to be told. I met so many people who let me into their lives. So many people who entrusted me with their stories. *I loved the challenge.*

Until one of those roller coaster twists jolted me. The joy went out of the career I had dreamed about since I was a kid. There were so many tough situations, so many sad stories. I put myself in the middle of them. To me, telling the true stories meant going into some places and situations my mom still doesn't know about. Murder scenes, homeless camps, police raids. In the end, it took its toll. My feelings got too heavy.

I took a sharp turn and went to the "dark side" of media relations. When a reporter becomes a PR professional, as many do, we call it "going to the dark side." Once on the receiving end of endless press releases, we were now charged with writing and distributing them in hopes of capturing a reporter's attention. After all, we should know what would jolt a reporter into action, right? I justified the twist in my career because I was doing it for a non-profit community clinic association. I was doing it for good. *I loved the meaning.*

After a few years, another turn. I was newly married and wanted a job with the opportunity to grow, where I could advance. We were a young couple, living on hope and looking for stability. We were a hard-working pair with a mortgage and plans to have a family. I was heading towards a new twist that would send me back into a familiar place.

My dad found the job in the newspaper classifieds. The supermarket I worked at during college was hiring an entry-level communications specialist. I remember him bringing over the ad, circled in red. He loved the company, so he was thrilled. And the thought of going back to a place where I felt like team equaled family, it excited me, too. I applied and kept my fingers crossed. They called me and, after three interviews, I got the job. It turns out they liked that I had reporting experience and, most importantly, store experience. I was in for a new, exciting ride.

I spent the next nine years there—moving from a specialist to a senior manager leading corporate communications. I professionally grew up there, learning what it meant to be corporate, but also holding on to my experience as a store employee. I never wanted to lose that perspective. It was the people in the stores who served the customers. Our job was to serve the store employees. *I loved the impact.*

During this time, I also learned that I lived somewhere in between marketing and HR. When corporate restructures happened, I would bounce between the two functions and my team would follow me. I am convinced they weren't sure where to put a former reporter who had learned skills on the job like talent review, succession planning, and organizational development. Heck, I wasn't sure either. So, I took those twists and turns until, one day in April 2010, the ride ended.

I will never forget that day. We were called to the company auditorium, department by department. The office was buzzing with rumors of a massive layoff. I was talking with a long-time friend and co-worker. He was saying, "It's not going to happen to you. They need you." In that moment, I looked down at my Blackberry. I had gotten the email to gather in the auditorium.

We sat in chairs arranged theater style. I had two female co-workers on either side of me. They were earlier in their careers. They were scared. I held their hands, gripping them tighter as the message was shared. I looked straight ahead, feeling like we were on a plane about to crash. I wanted to protect them, but I couldn't. I couldn't even protect myself or my own family.

The joy was sucked out of that building that day. The friend I was talking with just moments before getting that fated email was among several who met me on the first floor as I prepared to depart, with tears in his eyes. My best friend met me down the street at Starbucks so I could gather my thoughts before driving home. He was spared—but maybe not really—because he was among those left behind. The following weeks, months, and years were not easy for those who remained. They had lost 40% of their colleagues that day.

Three weeks after my layoff, I landed a job at a reputable healthcare system. I was so fortunate for the opportunity and learned a great deal there. But I couldn't help feeling like I was on the wrong ride, a mini roller coaster that didn't give me quite the same thrill. Plus, I felt like I had some unfinished work. I wanted to go back to the unpredictable and fast-paced world of grocery. Three years later, there was an opportunity to get on that oh-so-familiar ride again.

I got the call on an ordinary day. A leader I had worked with since the beginning of my corporate career wanted to introduce me to the new head of marketing. He needed someone to do internal and external communications. We had lunch. It went great. There was a chance I could return. I might be able to complete what I thought wasn't yet completed. And, well, my dad was even more ecstatic. At this point, he was ailing. I was following through for me, my family, and him.

I met the VP a second time at a store that I had helped open a few years earlier. He wrote my job description on the back of a napkin. He put everything in internal and external communications on a team with me. Organizational and employee communications. PR and social media. Customer response and events. Whoa!! This was seriously the job I had been wanting. Talk about exhilaration! Then, there was the wait. Like waiting in a loooooong line for that roller coaster you're dying to ride. It took about six months to make it happen. At that point, my dad's health was worsening. I swear one of the few things he was holding out for was for me to get that job offer. It finally came. We were both relieved.

My dad died six weeks later. He would not live to see that the girl who bagged groceries would eventually become a vice president for the same company. It happened three years after I returned. Now, this was my dream job. I was responsible for employee communication, leadership development, training and recruiting—the entire employee experience! And I took my responsibility seriously, sharing the employee perspective at the executive table.

I loved going to work. I had an incredible team. We were small, but mighty. We had fun AND got the work done. We were building culture, employee experience, and future leaders. We were going up, up, up! *I loved the purpose.*

Then, bam. The roller coaster took an upside down twist and launched downward. And it was a steep descent. It happened quickly yet felt like slo-mo. In a matter of a year, something changed. I was moved to another team, back to marketing again. I was game for the ride. In fact, I was excited for it. Who could have known it would be so different? All of a sudden, the woman who used to spring out of bed with the sound of the alarm clock didn't want to get up. I didn't want to go to work. The excitement was lost. I felt like I couldn't do anything right. I felt small and unnecessary. I felt judged and shamed. I knew the end was coming. I had to wait it out. The day I returned from vacation in January 2020, I was told goodbye and good luck.

It wasn't luck, but a network of caring and authentic professionals—mentors, coaches, friends—that helped me realize that I had something unique to offer the business world. I was uncertain and frightened. And then, I remembered the roller coaster. It wasn't the end. This was simply a dip. I would ascend back up again. It would be scary and thrilling at the same time. I was in for the ride. Heck, I was architecting this one. And it felt awesome!

After going to a few networking events and applying for some jobs, I had a friend ask me if I wanted to do a freelance project while looking for work. Totally! So, I launched a company from my mom's kitchen table. I let fate take control and rolled with it, transitioning from an employee to unemployed to self-employed. It was quite the ride! It took hard work, intention and resilience. I've learned a few things in this transition, building on what I've learned throughout my career:

1. **Leverage your connection with others.** We have the opportunity to make connections throughout our lives. Make them real and make them matter. Be there for others for the right reasons, and they will be there for you when you need them most. Don't be afraid to ask for support and help.

2. **Take on challenge with realistic positivity.** We will all face challenges, particularly when making changes in our lives. Know what you're heading into, but also recognize your strength will get you through it. Your outlook can make the difference as to whether you persevere through transition.

3. **Prioritize what means most to you.** Understand what matters to you. Do you prioritize making an impact over making money? Do you want flexibility at work more than you want daily connection with peers? Considering and prioritizing what means most to you in your work can help you find the right role.

4. **Define how you will make an impact.** Think about what making an impact looks like to you. Your impact is your legacy—and it is a big question to consider. If you define how you want to make a difference in the world, you will better understand what you are "meant to do."

5. **Know and live your purpose.** You may work for a company that has a defined purpose, but what is your personal purpose? If you can articulate what makes you excited to get out of bed, what is even a bit scary and exhilarating to you, then you've likely found it. Put it to work.

Today, my purpose is making work count for employees and businesses. Why? The joy of work comes from people enjoying their work—finding connection and challenge, realizing their meaning and impact, and being able to live their purpose. I will always believe this—because I've lived it myself. The ups, the downs, the turnarounds. I will continue my adrenalin-pumping ride, both exciting and scary at the same time. I will take the twists and turns any day, because each one makes me better and brings me closer to realizing my strength, perseverance, and potential. And that's what makes a ride of a lifetime.

Nicole Townsend

Nicole Townsend founded her professional consulting firm in 2020 to make work count for employees and businesses. Experience Counts develops and implements strategies that make an impact across the employee experience by strengthening culture, engagement and results.

With 20 years of experience in human resources and marketing, she brings her clients a unique perspective that connects the employee and customer experience with business results. Her clients span the retail, restaurant, manufacturing, and healthcare industries.

Prior to starting her own firm, Nicole was the vice president of team member experience at Raley's, a West Sacramento-based grocery chain. She aligned strategy and content across employee touch points from pre-hire to retire. She led recruiting, communication, learning solutions and employee development. Nicole was on the organization's Executive Steering Committee and was honored as a Top Woman in Grocery by Progressive Grocer magazine in 2016. She served as a Trustee on the California Grocers Association Educational Foundation board.

As an entrepreneur, Nicole is involved with organizations that support small business. She is a member of the National Organization of Women Owned Business (NAWBO), which nominated her for an Outstanding Women Leader award for "Women on the Way" in 2022. She supports BOLD, an annual women's speaker series based in Sacramento. She takes part in classes by the Carlsen Center for Innovation at her alma mater, CSU, Sacramento, where she graduated with a degree in journalism.

Nicole lives in the Sacramento area with her husband of 20+ years, their two teen-aged children, and their adored Pomeranian poodle.

Connect with Nicole at www.experiencecounts.us.

CHAPTER 15

3 Ps Wrapped in an E

by Pam Marcheski

Beginning my reflection for writing this chapter, I turned to what is one of my most important daily practices, meditation. Meditation has become a cornerstone of how I live my life. It wasn't always; meditation only became part of my daily routine in the last seven to eight years and was found during a time in my career when I wasn't feeling much joy. I knew I had a pretty good leadership toolbox, but the box wasn't opening as efficiently as it used to. The practice of meditation taught me how to open the leadership toolbox of my mind, as I like to say.

In the beginning, my meditation practice was simply a few moments of intentional breathing before heading into a meeting or a store that I was visiting, a few minutes of sitting and contemplating my intention for the next interaction I was to have. Those brief moments of breathing and reflection gave me what I needed to show up more effectively and more wholeheartedly into my interactions, even when it was possibly going to be difficult. As I began to see the impact that these minor moments of practice had on myself, and more importantly how I was showing up for others, I began to extend my practice to longer periods of time.

Years later, meditation is now a cornerstone in my life and the work I do. The practice has given me access to a much more joyful personal and professional life.

The meditation practice I chose to contemplate in this chapter is a death contemplation meditation. The death contemplation is taught in many of the most ancient mindfulness traditions and one I find to be incredibly beautiful and powerful. There are several different ways one can do this meditation. In this one, I sat for several hours over many days and reflected on the impermanence of everything as guidance for living life fully and the beauty of that. Meditation, and particularly the death contemplation meditation, has reinforced a guidance I remind myself and others to hold it light. Frank Ostaseski, international Buddhist teacher and cofounder of the Zen Hospice Center shared, "It is an absurd gamble to wait until the time of death to learn the lessons it must teach us. Keeping death at your fingertips reminds us that life is a precious and precarious thing. You lighten up and you stop holding things so tightly."

Death was introduced as a possibility very early on in my life. At age thirteen, on an average spring day, my fourteen-year-old brother and I went to school together, but by that evening I was an only child. My brother had a sudden heart attack at school that day and while everyone did what they could to save him, he passed within hours. Our family very suddenly learned the truth about the essence of impermanence and how it can be revealed at any time. So, the death contemplation meditation came easily for me. Culturally, in the west, death is conditioned to be something we push away from and move away from and therefore this meditation can sometimes be disturbing. However, when embraced, death can reveal some beautiful possibilities of ways in which you guide your life's actions.

I sat for quite some time in silence reflecting and contemplating what the essence of my life would be if there were no tomorrow or even not one more hour. I sat with the Koan, who am I at work when I die. A Koan is a deeper reflective question that we can sit with in meditation for a very long time, in some cases years. A Koan provokes the removing of logic and reasoning to provoke deeper wisdom for us. Who I am at work when I die led me to my three Ps wrapped together with an E: Purpose, People, Play and Effort.

Here is what my time in reflection has brought to me, related to work and joy.

PURPOSE: Growing up, I went on many drives with my father. During those rides, there were times where my father pointed out a building and shared with me, "See that Pammy, I was part of building that." My dad would always smile, and I felt a sense of pride in him as he shared. My father, a tough guy brought up on the streets of Detroit and a sheet metal worker, taught me at a very early age how important purpose was in work. He taught me that when you can build a connection between the work you are doing to something bigger there was a great deal of joy.

Throughout my career, the purpose theme was something I lived and hoped I still lead. I always found a meaning and purpose in every job. That includes my four years as a fast-food guru for Taco Bell. I loved the challenge of making food for people and never thought it was beneath me to make fast food. Early in my retail career, I worked in the back room by myself and oversaw receiving and processing all of the product. I found purpose there as well; I loved the challenge of getting the merchandise to the retail floor, because I knew if I did this well, customers could buy it and the store would have great success.

As a leader, purpose and meaning were important in how I guided and led. I loved visiting the back rooms and cheering on the teams and making sure they knew they were part of something big. I loved being in stores and always hoped to leave people with the understanding that, we don't win if you don't win.

PEOPLE: The second reveal to me during my death contemplation was people. This was revealed to me reflecting again on growing up, this time with my mom and her work. Mom was an insurance agent, she worked independently with her clients while her coworkers worked with their clients. Mom always seemed to build strong friendships and connections. Her coworkers became friends who often became family. My mom taught me that while she worked alone, people around her mattered and that having a connection to people made a big difference in the joy she experienced at work. Mom never really spoke about the big client or big deal she closed, but she sure brought to life the understanding that connection to people was important.

People have been everything in my work both now and the decades of time spent in retail stores. Early on as a department manager, I made deep close friendships with those I worked with. At that time, there was a greater cultivation of this in stores. Breakroom parties, holiday parties and engaging outside of work wasn't the big taboo it seems to be today. I feel sad for people today who work alone, take breaks alone, and have a culture that doesn't put resources into cultivating people and relationships.

As a leader, I hope people on the teams I led knew they were most important to me, beyond anything else. My field team had lunches together, we met weekly together and when possible, we traveled together. We shared about our personal lives, laughed about recent encounters in our travels, and spent many hours sitting and waiting for a delayed flight. Working with friends has been shown to be one of the highest levels of engagement in an organization. I am deeply grateful for those relationships that have come into my life and that continue to appear through my work.

PLAY: The third reveal in my death contemplation was play. Death contemplation can feel very heavy and there is a seriousness to the contemplation, but then you test the opposite of death and grieving and find play and joy. One cannot feel the power of grief if you haven't felt joy.

I learned the value of play from some of my earliest tough high-charging leaders who still found ways to have fun and play. I learned through their example that high standards and the drive for results come at the highest level when you find ways to keep it light and fun for those you are leading. I also learned the opposite from other leaders who didn't emulate any feelings of fun and play; their team environment was more tense and guarded and results waned.

Play can be inside and outside of actual work, but the culture of lightness and play inside is essential if you are leading others. It is there, in the sometimes silliness that people can find the greatest psychological safety and vulnerability. If a company or leader operates with tightness while working and only offers play when work is done or in special circumstances, the impact is lost and often because moments of obligation for employees to attend. I sometimes guided my more serious leaders with the quip -hokey works- as a guidepost and reminder that sometimes we must just let our hair down.

Early on, play was harder for me. Finding my way as a young female progressing her career there was an uneasiness in showing the silly and I likely lost moments where I could have done better for those I was leading. Thankfully I moved through that discomfort and ensured that play and lightness were felt within my teams, even during our hard-charging and serious times.

All of these... Purpose, People and Play... were in my reflection, but it wasn't complete. There was something missing and that was **EFFORT**...there is no effort in dying, but there is real effort in living. We live much of our lives at work, therefore effort and what makes it joyful, deserves some consideration.

According to the Oxford Dictionary the definition of work is to exert physical or mental energy to accomplish a goal. Exertion takes effort... so if the goal is to have joyful work, there will have to be effort. Things that matter take effort, is a regular phrase I share with everyone, this just makes sense for me.

Every job can have a purpose, but there are jobs that at times will take more effort to find a sense of connection bigger than the task at hand. This is personal effort, not the meaning or culture of the company. My inner most personal purpose gave me the motivation to do my best, regardless of the role I was in.

People take an effort. Relationships can be challenging and that doesn't change in work or in life. Relationships must be cultivated to thrive and often the demands of the job can collide with the perception of time and getting things done.

Play can take effort. Play when the work at hand is serious and needs to be done can leave one to forgo play. Intentional effort is needed to keep the work playful and light. It is in the place of light and playfulness where work can flourish.

Two things that never came up during my death contemplation meditation and reflecting on my Koan, Who am I at work when I die? These were money and title.

Money did not show up. To be clear, being paid fairly for the work I did was certainly important to me, particularly in the early years of my career as a single mom raising my son alone. Paying for daycare and everything else a child requires was on my mind with the highest urgency. Money was essential to take care of the external needs of life, and while important, these demands ebb and flow. Long ago, one of those leaders that I put on the not so good list encouraged us to celebrate and encourage those I led to buy lots of things with the money they earned. In his mind, this would keep them staying and working hard. Hearing his guidance was actually good because it provided clarity to me that I never wanted to live that way personally and I did not want to lead my team in this way. By not following this guidance, I was empowered to change my career and my life several times.

The title also never came forward for me. In meditation we teach the concept of non-identification. The understanding that when thoughts, emotions and in descriptions such as titles become who we are suffering is likely. Titles can be necessary to define roles and responsibilities in a company but when the title becomes our worth the risk of suffering is there.

Working hard and moving your role forward are deeply rewarding. I worked hard and I was certainly proud when I got my first store and again when I became a Vice President. I am proud to own my company today. But those moments with a title are short. The magic of what was in front of my name then and now quickly loses its luster. What never gets old is waking up and knowing my purpose, connecting to others, and getting to play and have fun.

Money and Title are external factors that can be positive rewards for the work one does but are unreliable as a source of real sustainable joy. What we hold externally will be susceptible to comparison, to protecting, to wanting, and to separating from others. In this space, we evoke emotions that are unhealthy. Emotions such as fear, anxiety, depression all lie heavily in the external and in separation from others. Purpose, People and Play cultivated with effort are internal and anything one builds internally is empowering, enduring, and evokes our most positive emotions (joy being one of the most prominent). History, science, philosophy, and psychological studies show very consistently to have joy, real joy that is sustainable and enduring, you must build from the inside out and not the other way around.

Who am I at work when I die? The Koan I began with revealed in contemplation - Three Ps wrapped with an E. I have found joy in work through my meditations. I've discovered how purpose, people, play and effort all have a place in filling my day with joy. Finding those 3 Ps wrapped with an E made all the difference.

"Of all the footprints, that of the elephant is supreme. Similarly, of all mindfulness meditation, that on death is supreme." ~The Buddha

---

Pam Marcheski

Pam Marcheski is the principal owner of Intentions to Actions Leadership. A Mindfulness-based leadership company that centers around helping individuals and organizations identify their desired leadership intentions in personal and professional life. With the structure of utilizing the traditional leadership development model combined with the foundations of mindfulness, Pam helps to guide a roadmap with actions that align with those intentions.

Pam spent the first twenty-five years of her career as a senior-level executive within several Fortune 500 companies. She employs her experience of leading teams with over 1,000 employees and P&L responsibility for billions of dollars in business, to now coach individuals and organizations in operational excellence, leadership development, and organizational strategy and implementation.

In her coaching approach, Pam utilizes her past experience and multiple certifications, including Mindfulness Performance and Awareness Coaching, obtained through the University of California San Diego, and Marshall Goldsmith's Stakeholder Centered Coaching and Strength-Based Coaching. She brings practical, real-life experience to the forefront and meets her client's needs wherever they are. She is a certified Executive and Organizational Leadership Coach that has a passion for helping leaders and organizations get to the next level while linking their intentions to action through customized coaching engagements.

Pam is an active member of the Harvard Medical School-affiliated Institute of Coaching, SHRM, and Women's Leadership Institute, where she volunteers, speaks, and collaborates with others on the latest leadership and organizational needs.

Pam lives and thrives in her community of San Diego, California, and has the pleasure of residing close to her adult son.

Connect with Pam at www.intentact.com.

CHAPTER 16

How I Moved from an "Accidental" Vocation to the Work I Love Most

by Robert Hilliard

When people ask me how I became an executive coach, I tell them that it happened by "accident." I use that word on purpose because it fits my experience perfectly. Merriam-Webster Dictionary defines an accident as an unforeseen and unplanned event or circumstance, which sums up my entire working experience. Let me explain. Music was my first love and the only thing that I wanted to do for as long as I can remember. It was my mission and having a mission was tremendously helpful. It guided my learning through high school, college, and beyond. This singular focus proved to be a liability because, as it turns out, making ends meet as a musician is pretty tough. So, like many aspiring musicians, I got a day job to balance things out. I deliberately took a role in an organization that allowed me to keep in sight my goal of making music. After years of balancing my passion and my day job, I decided to look for a career that I could enjoy and be financially secure. That proved harder than I anticipated. So, I made the difficult decision to put my music career on hold and resigned myself to the predictable grind of my day job. That is, until the day my manager called me into his office for an unscheduled meeting.

As I waited, I began to tick off a list of things that I must have done wrong. Why else would he want to see me? Try as I might, I couldn't think of anything. After what seemed like an eternity, he called me in. I didn't have to wait long to hear what he wanted. The meeting had nothing to do with my performance. As it turned out, my manager was scheduled to facilitate a workshop in our Dallas office. Summers in Texas can be brutal, and he just didn't want to go, so he had arranged for me to take his place! To prepare, I created a training outline and reviewed it with him. Eager to do a decent job, I threw myself into the assignment and did well. In fact, I did so well that word spread throughout the organization and, before long, I was being requested to do workshops in other parts of the country. Before I knew it, I had a new career as a trainer. I stayed in that position for two years. And when my manager left for a job in a bank's call center, he took me with him. Oddly enough, he left the bank a year later, but I stayed on.

My skills grew at the bank and shortly thereafter I became the "go to" person for interpersonal skills and management training. I enjoyed my work, and the participants enjoyed my courses, but I seldom felt that I was making a real impact. Something was missing. Then, one day it hit me: the work that I was doing didn't help others further *their* aspirations. I shared my thinking with my new boss. After giving this some thought, she stated that perhaps I should stretch out of my comfort zone a bit. She went on to share her vision, which included showcasing my skills in a more visible way. Per the plan, she arranged for me to take her place in some important executive meetings. However, despite my best efforts, I couldn't get senior executives to buy into my ideas. Some humored me, stating that they admired my "enthusiasm," but felt my thinking was a bit "forward" for the organization. Others blatantly questioned my boss's decision to include me in the meetings. Their argument was that since I was good at what I did, she should keep me firmly rooted in my position. Before long, it became apparent that advancing my career at the bank was not likely. So, my boss suggested another strategy: acquire more knowledge and skill and then move on. In her opinion, I had enough talent to run an entire employee development department, but that wasn't going to happen at the bank. She felt that in order for me to be truly successful, I needed to get very clear on my career goals and create a strategy to reach them. She asked, "What's your plan?" Her question brought me up a little short. As incredible as it sounds, I hadn't ever thought to create my own plan. Until that moment, I was content to hitch my wagon to my boss, work hard, and let their success carry me. (In retrospect, that was an awful plan.) I was truly stumped. After what seemed like an eternity of silence, she sent me on my way, but, before I reached the door, she warned me that she would give me two weeks to come up with an answer. The only thing that I knew for sure was that I wanted to have a bigger impact on people, but I had no idea how to do it.

These types of sessions became routine over the next several months: my boss would ask me questions about my goals and challenges, then task me with finding a plan or a solution. It was tedious, but over time, a plan started to form. I would hone my existing skills, look for any gaps that I had, use my available resources to gain more knowledge, and volunteer for projects that showcased my abilities. This strategy worked extremely well and, after two years, I moved on to a health-care organization that I felt was more in line with my core values. This new organization promoted itself as "innovative" and "cutting edge." Unfortunately, when I began working there, I realized that it was neither. However, it *did* have a lot of people that needed help.

The pace at my new organization was the opposite of the one at the bank. At the bank, my work moved in a controlled, methodical fashion. However, my new organization required me to hit the ground running. In the first meeting with my new boss, he told me that the organization's frontline employees had gone years without any soft skills training whatsoever. He continued by explaining that there also hadn't been any training courses on managerial skills. This was shocking enough, but the real stunner was his statement that "quality was second to quantity." In fact, my mandate was to design and facilitate as many courses as I could as quickly as I was able. After I gathered myself, I told him that I could design and facilitate the courses, but that I was not comfortable just throwing something together. Instead, I proposed that I be allowed to design training that would be truly impactful for the participants. After going back and forth for a bit, I got him to reluctantly agree to my plan. Within five years, I had not only designed and facilitated the organization's first management training program but launched a suite of programs for frontline staff as well. The crown jewel was a leadership training program that, for the first time, helped create career paths for frontline employees who wanted to grow in the organization. However, my boss never stopped throwing me curve balls.

Soon after the launch of these programs, my boss called me into his office for an impromptu meeting. After we exchanged a few pleasantries, he said, "I think that you'd be a great executive coach. What do you think about doing some coaching in the organization?" Not wanting to turn down an opportunity, I agreed. "Great," he said. "I have a candidate already lined up for you. Here's their email. Contact them and schedule some sessions by the end of the week!" "Um, okay," was all I could muster before shuffling out of his office. Despite explaining my work process on every project thus far, my boss still believed that quantity was more important than quality. However, I had already agreed to do the sessions, so I decided to give it my best.

Having no idea how to facilitate a successful coaching session, I prepared by reading a book on coaching and creating a list of questions that I was certain would create brilliant "aha" moments for my client. After all, I had been coached once or twice before. The people that coached me seemed to easily navigate those sessions. How hard could it be? Pretty hard, it turned out. I was able to at least provide an empathetic ear for the client, but, by the end of those sessions, it was clear that if I was to be any good, I needed solid training. With that, I went in search of a coach training school. Within a week, I was enrolled and committed to my learning. I spent the next nine months learning everything I could about coaching and came to realize that it was one of the best career decisions I ever made.

It didn't take me long to realize that coaching was a natural complement to my employee development duties. It was especially helpful as an "add on" to my training workshops. For example, instead of just giving "remedial" training to employees who were having difficulty transferring skills to their jobs, I employed a coaching approach that allowed employees to design their own solutions. This was met with incredible enthusiasm. For the first time, employees felt committed to applying what they learned in the classroom, because they finally had a say in how things could be done. Their enthusiasm affected me profoundly. For the first time in my career, I felt like I was truly making a difference. This translated to a sense of gratitude when I thought about my job duties. It turned out that coaching was the missing piece for which I'd been searching. Feeling re-energized, I decided to give executive coaching another try, but with a twist. After using my newly acquired coaching skills with frontline employees, I was confident that coaching could be effective with the entire leadership team. So, I proposed an internal coaching program that was open to all leaders in the organization. This required a shift in thinking for senior executives because they only saw coaching as a way to assist those who were struggling. It took some effort, but I was able to convince them. The program launched in 2011 and remained in place until I left the organization in 2020. Leaving the organization was difficult, but I embraced the change.

Clients often remark on the changes that they see in themselves. I'm not surprised by this. After all, coaching works. Thinking back on my career, I see the unexpected changes coaching had on me. Through coaching others, I learned to listen deeply, connect with empathy, and deal with strong emotions. I developed the habit of reframing negative events so that they reflect positive possibilities. This shift in thinking now helps me view setbacks as opportunities for growth. Perhaps the most noticeable change I see is the overall awareness of myself. Prior to becoming a coach, I typically only reflected on my behavior when someone else brought it to my attention. Through coaching (and tons of practice), I gained the ability to observe my thinking in a way that allows me to respond thoughtfully. These changes help facilitate the deep sense of connection that was long missing in my career. It is, perhaps, because of these changes that I now have a new attitude toward "accidents" and "mistakes." Today when I work with clients, I often remind them that accidents are often necessary to build skill. In order to build skill, you must look at them like messages alerting you that adjustments are needed. Of course, not all accidents are beneficial. However, if you can shift your perspective, a bit, you may be able to see new possibilities. Embracing this way of thinking allows me to view every confusing, frustrating experience in my career as natural obstacles on the path that led me to the career that I love.

Robert Hilliard

Conscious, energetic, and collaborative is how Robert Hilliard describes his coaching approach. He often tells his clients that having a coach doubles their brainpower. Like a computer with extra processing capabilities, the access to additional perspectives helps people to see solutions they didn't know existed. When different perspectives are explored, new and exciting breakthroughs occur.

Robert is a graduate of the Institute for Professional Excellence in Coaching (iPEC) with the designations of Certified Professional Coach, Energy Leadership Index Master Practitioner, and COR.E Leadership Dynamics Specialist. He also holds a master's degree in Organizational Development and Leadership from Saint Joseph's University.

Robert's passion for coaching comes from his desire to help others achieve goals they didn't think were possible. He does this by drawing on his 25 years of experience in the field of Organizational Development working in the entertainment, finance, and healthcare industries. Robert prides himself on helping others get better results with less stress. In fact, helping clients remove the stress that blocks creative energy is one of the core principles of his coaching process. He has helped clients navigate difficult conversations, build effective teams, broaden their professional network, apply new leadership methods, and enhance their leadership presence.

Robert is a life-long New Yorker. When not coaching, he likes to spend time with his family and pursue his passions for music, photography, and martial arts.

Connect with Robert at www.roberthilliardcoaching.com.

Finding Joy

by Sally Green

How do you define "work"? Is it the job you're paid to do? Or is it the actions you take to achieve your goals?

Where is the Joy?

Throughout my life, I've worked at many jobs. I worked in a factory after school typing purchase orders, I worked in a machine shop scheduling parts for production. I worked in a computer sales company as an inventory specialist and for the past 28 years, I have owned and operated my own housecleaning business. While I was good at those jobs and they provided financial support, they didn't bring me joy or fulfillment.

During my 20s, I took on a part-time job that I truly en-JOY-ed. I sold skincare and make-up at home parties and worked as a makeup artist. I have always had a fascination with the art of makeup and the way it could make someone feel confident and look beautiful. There was nothing that brought me greater joy than being able to help women feel pretty and special, especially for weddings and other special events.

Unfortunately, the job was with a multi-level marketing company and, while I was one of the top saleswomen in Connecticut, I was not a recruiter. The pay was not enough to allow me to leave my full-time job, and once my daughter was born, I made the difficult decision to stop selling makeup and start my own house-cleaning business.

I absolutely loved teaching skincare and makeup application! The smiles and happiness that came with helping women find their perfect look and feel more confident will always hold a special place in my heart.

It would be another 28 years before I found another job that I loved as much.

Finding Joy in Teaching

When I was 26, the minister at my church asked if I would teach Sunday School. Teaching was something I had always loved. After praying about it, I approached the head of Christian Education and volunteered to teach. That was the beginning of a 30-year career teaching Sunday School. Creating and teaching lessons about faith to kids was a source of joy for me. Although there were challenges, teaching Sunday School provided me with valuable insights about teaching, children, and myself. Despite not having enough volunteer teachers and low class attendance, I persevered. Most of the time we had a one-room classroom setting. At times, I found it difficult trying to teach children at different ages and reading levels. But I had a passion for researching the Bible stories and I discovered my faith grew as I taught. Teaching and leading Sunday School brought me so much joy! I finally retired back in 2018 and to be honest, I've missed it ever since. What can I say? It's hard to let go of something you love doing so much!

After I stepped away from teaching Sunday school, I found myself leading and writing Bible Studies for women. Since that time, I have authored three bible studies and found that writing has become a new-found passion. My walk with God has been an incredible adventure and I'm eager to see what He has in store for me next.

Finding Joy in Art

My daughter left for college when I was 50, and I became an empty nester. One thing I discovered during that time was my passion for painting. I attended a Paint and Sip event one Friday night with some friends, and I loved it so much that I went out the next day and purchased canvases, paintbrushes, and paint. I loved the fact that regardless of my painting ability, I was able to lose myself in the moment and relieve stress when I painted.

I began taking online art classes a few nights a week. Soon, I was creating my own little masterpieces in the living room! When my friends saw my paintings, they wanted to join in the fun too. I started hosting my own paint nights in my home, providing paint supplies and snacks for my friends.

Soon after, I found myself teaching art classes and absolutely loving it. It was then that I decided to take it to the next level. In January 2020, I made the leap to turn painting into a business by offering "paint and wine" nights. I created a business plan, reached out to family and friends, and began working to formalize a schedule. My church allowed me to use their basement for monthly painting classes. Everything was set to go, and I kicked off my classes in January of 2020. In March, the pandemic hit, forcing me to cancel all my sessions. In April, the huge fundraiser I had scheduled called and canceled because of covid restrictions, I was devastated!

I discovered that whenever I am feeling down or emotional, painting always cheers me up. It's amazing to see how all my feelings get woven into my art - from my hands to the brush to the canvas. Painting still makes me so happy, especially when a blank canvas comes alive with my brushstrokes!

Finding Joy in Writing

Our life experiences, both good and bad, shape us for what's yet to come. Change is inevitable, yet it's how we mature and progress. And as we go through life, we have the power to help others do the same. We can all make an impact on the world, but it starts with committing to personal growth. That's when everything falls into place; we become more confident, stronger and better equipped to handle whatever life throws our way!

When the pandemic hit and I couldn't teach art classes, I became depressed. I knew I had to do something different. I embarked on a journey of self-care and self-discovery. I began eating healthier and taking daily walks with my husband and daughter. I shut off the television and read self-improvement books instead. I began my mornings with meditation and prayer. One evening I was offered the opportunity to write a chapter in a collaboration book on entrepreneurship. I jumped at the chance and began looking for ways to leverage the opportunity. I started reaching out to the other authors in the book and began connecting with them. I registered for their online courses, joined summits they were speaking at, and attended networking events they were hosting. I made sure to raise my hand and ask questions in Zoom rooms, so they knew who I was.

I was so excited to write in my first collaboration book, that I quickly signed up for another one. It was through that process that I met Lynda Sunshine West. Her weekly networking events became a regular for me, and I soon registered for her business masterclass. Lynda graciously extended the opportunity for me to write chapters in two books she was publishing, and I gladly accepted. Within a year, I had written chapters in four #1 International bestselling collaboration books – it was a dream come true!

Finding Joy in Publishing

Something amazing happened after my books were published. People began reaching out to me, sharing their own stories. It was completely overwhelming and humbling to realize that my story could touch the hearts of others. The next thing I knew, Lynda offered me the opportunity to join her in the publishing business. I was thrilled! We were both passionate about providing aspiring writers with a platform to share their stories. I believe that everyone's story matters, and I am absolutely determined to help people find their voices and share their stories with the world!

Together we started publishing collaboration books and have designed workshops and coaching programs to guide writers through the publishing process. It's wonderful to learn the publishing process from the inside and witness how individuals transform when they write and share their stories.

I received other opportunities too! I was invited to speak on various online summits, discussing my experiences and encouraging others to embrace their own stories. Over the past few years, I've stepped out of my comfort zone several times. It has been nerve-wracking at times, but I have persevered.

I've come to realize that my purpose in life is to help others discover the power of their own stories. I'm grateful for the opportunities that have come my way, the friendships I've formed, and all the surprises along the way. Life is unpredictable, but I'm ready to embrace it with open arms and an open heart.

My days are filled with joy in publishing books and helping others bring their stories to life. I've realized that investing in myself was key to discovering my purpose and finding joy. It wasn't a piece of cake, but it was worth every moment!

As part of the Publishing Company, we have built a community of supportive writers. We celebrate their successes, offer guidance during challenges, and provide a safe place for their creativity to bloom. And you know what's amazing? All the friendships that have blossomed along the way - a true blessing! The best part of all this is being able to witness the transformative power of storytelling first-hand. I've witnessed people heal from past wounds; find strength to overcome obstacles and inspire others with their courage. The impact of words goes way beyond the pages of a book.

Finding Joy in Life

It's crazy to think about how far I've come in the past twelve years. I started off as an Empty Nester searching for a way to be creative and now, I'm a book publisher who is empowering writers to share their stories. It's been an incredible journey full of growth and fulfillment!

Don't ever doubt the power of your own experiences and how they can impact others. Your voice and story are one-of-a-kind! Exploring your passion is a journey worth taking. Take time to explore your interests, seek opportunities for growth, and surround yourself with like-minded people who uplift and inspire you. Embrace sharing your story with the world, through writing, speaking, or any medium you choose. It is through our unique stories that we inspire and connect with others, leaving a lasting impact on those around us. You have the power to make a positive impact on the world. So, invest in yourself, step out of your comfort zone, let your story unfold, and embrace the Joy you find along the way!

IF

by Sally Larkin Green

If fresh flowers bloomed in my garden all year,
If I could make a wish and you would appear,
If I could eat what I want and never get fat,
If a kitten would never become a cat,

If I could exercise once and be fit and lean,
If my kitchen and bathroom would keep itself clean,
If I could stay up late without falling asleep,
If my mug full of coffee was six feet deep,

If my laundry would wash and fold itself,
If chocolate kept appearing upon my shelf,
If thinking of you would make the sun shine,
If my bathtub was filled with bottles of wine ....

Now, THAT would make me happy!

Sally Green

Sally Green Is the Vice President of Author Development at Action Takers Publishing. She works with writers to help them develop their stories and become bestselling authors. Action Takers Publishing specializes in themed multi-author collaboration books where each person writes a chapter and becomes part of a community of like-minded authors. In addition to collaboration books, they also published solo books

At the age of 58, Sally realized that she was really good at taking care of everyone else, but really bad at taking care of herself. So, she embarked on a journey of self-care that began with investing in herself and contributing to a multi-author book. Sally is an inspirational speaker, a multiple times International Bestselling Author and is in the process of writing her own book titled: The Self-Care Rockstar due to launch in 2023.

Connect with Sally at www.actiontakerspublishing.com.

CHAPTER 18

What if...?

by Shelly Buettner

As a little kid, were you drawn to any specific career topics or have certain things you gravitated towards without knowing why?

Did you pretend to be a nurse or firefighter, dressing up in your 'job-gear' and prancing around putting out fires or helping to heal people with your toy stethoscope?

Do you believe your childhood interests can fuel your adult career decisions and spark joy inside of you?

I do. And here's why.

Are you doing anything in your work as an adult that lit you up as a child, or did you select your career by doing things you thought you were supposed to do – like going to college, getting the job everyone said you'd be good at, and leaving it at that?

We have all met someone we see as successful and happy, and they say, "Yeah, I always wanted to be a Whatchamacallit when I grew up, and here I am. I'm a successfully, happy Whatchamacallit!" And you reply, "Oh, my gosh, how cool! That sounds fantastic!" Then they ask you what you do, and in the cheeriest voice you can muster, you tell them you're a monotonous hum drummer at the local humdrummery. Yeah – don't laugh. It happens.

Childhood interests can certainly influence our adult decisions, even subconsciously. We all know people like the successful Whatchamacallit person. I believe that as children, we may know our most authentic selves better than we may think. I also believe that with some thought, retrospection, and by asking ourselves the right questions, we can home in on our natural talents and interests that fuel our soul.

Think about this for a minute...

As children, we were allowed to pretend, be anything we wanted, and play without restrictions. The sky was the limit when we were kids, and there wasn't anything we couldn't pretend to do or be, and we were happy pretending.

Yet as adults, so many of us get stuck in jobs that suck the life out of us and, sadly, we still pretend. We pretend everything is okay, and this is how it should be. We pretend we're fine.

I understand we sometimes have to do jobs we don't like or want to do to make ends meet, but do you enjoy what you do now?

If you answered "no," or thought, "Well, I'm kinda happy, and I like the money I earn, but my job really doesn't light a fire under my bum, and I can think of a few things I'd rather be doing," then maybe it's time to figure out what you like to do and if you want to do that instead of what you're doing now.

I fell into the trap of being a monotonous hum drummer at the local humdrummery. I know what it means to feel unfulfilled, bored, or frustrated with your employment or work environment. This feeling stinks. I need something that sparks my many interests – which can be diverse – something that lets me be creative and allows me to help people in some capacity.

Let's play a little game right now. It's an exercise in finding your joy.

Whether it's the joy of your work or what you're interested in and love in general, if you do this exercise, you may find joy all around – including in your career. When I did this exercise, I discovered I was following my joy in my work - without even realizing it!

Okay, here we go. I will share three little bits of information from my childhood with you.

#1 - The little girl in me loved jewelry

When I was 4 or 5 years old, I remember going to my grandma's house, and the first place I would run to was her bedroom dresser, where her jewelry box sat center stage! I would open it, listen to the music play, and stare at the beautiful diamonds and pearls inside. Of course, they weren't natural diamonds or genuine pearls, but I didn't know this then. I would reach my hands inside, take out a diamond necklace, and place it around my neck. Then I would decorate my ears with her screw-on clip pearl and diamond earrings and try to make her black and white cameo ring sit upon my tiny fingers without falling off.

I would pose in the mirror and talk to myself like I was the Queen of England, for goodness sakes. I did this for hours. It never got boring, and it always made me feel like a million bucks – even though I had no real concept of money at four years old.

My grandmother died when I was in either the 3rd or 4th grade. I was sad because I would not see her anymore or eat her yummy cookies from the large, green glass cookie jar. I was sad because what on God's earth was going to happen to her jewelry box with all those lovely jewels that reminded me of her and made me feel so beautiful and happy? Thankfully, I was gifted my grandmother's jewelry box and most of the jewelry inside when she passed. (How on earth did my family know this would have a profound effect on me later in life?)

Every time I open her jewelry box, I can still see my little 5-year-old image reflected in her mirror, draped in all those fine jewels. And I still believe I look like a million dollars when I put on her jewelry – even if it's still just for pretend. But what's not for pretend is the impact the jewelry in that box has had on my life.

I'm glad I didn't lose the ability to pretend or talk to myself. These traits have come in handy in my adult life and the career where I've found the most joy.

#2 – As a young girl, I loved to read and wanted to be a writer when I grew up

I would grab the newspaper in the 5th or 6th grade and read Irma Bombeck's column before school. For those of you who are too young to know – Google® her. She was funny and forward-thinking for the time. She sprinkled in witty humor and touched upon relevant and current issues – mainly as they pertained to housewives of the late 1960s. She opened my eyes to humorous writing. And to women's rights (or lack thereof, as the case was).

My sixth-grade English teacher, Mrs. Reynolds, encouraged and nurtured all of us kids with our writing. I wrote many poems and short stories, but I mainly wanted to write humorous articles like Irma

Bombeck. As luck would have it, Mrs. Reynolds let my friend Lisa and I write the Junior High School paper column, 'Dear Gabby.' Looking back, it made me feel a little more like Irma. I kept writing poems into my high school years. I wrote about teenage love and loss, my father's battle with cancer, and how I felt after his death during my sophomore year. When I thought no one else understood my feelings, writing was my sanctuary, and I could pour my heart out on the page and sit with it. Just me, the paper, my words and the Universe. No judgment.

I had no idea how this craft of writing would impact my life – personally and professionally.

#3 – I loved seeing the world through a camera lens as a young girl

My dad was a rural letter carrier, and we would go to the annual Rural Letter Carrier convention in the summer as our vacation. We would get up at the ungodly hour of 3:00 A.M., hit the road, and drive for hours upon hours across the country.

Dad didn't let us play the radio, and no car games were allowed to be played in the car either when Dad was driving. I would get bored or car sick from reading and say, "I'm bored!" My dad would respond with, "Look out the window. How can you be bored with this scenery?" So, I looked out the window.

As we drove, there were mountains, large trees, and sunny skies with big, puffy white clouds out the car window. Being a Central Illinois kid, I usually only had corn fields to look at, and it seemed always to be overcast or cloudy, so yes, this was beautiful scenery – Dad was right.

The pretty scenery spawned my desire to photograph what I saw. I wanted to capture the beauty and remember it. I asked for a camera for my next birthday so I could take pictures on vacation. My parents thought I was too irresponsible to have a new camera, so they gave me this old Kodak® Brownie Hawkeye Box camera my stepmom had. Nevertheless, it was a camera, and I was happy.

I staged this little stuffed puppy I named Fuzzy Waddles (no judging here, okay. I was only about nine years old at this point) on top of my dresser, beneath the cherry tree, on top of the car hood, on the stairs of the porch, in the willow tree branches, you name it. Fuzzy Waddles was everywhere, almost like Flat Stanley.

I practiced my photography because I wanted my vacation pictures to be perfect. I spent all my allowance getting the film developed. I loved taking pictures of Fuzzy Waddles. He looked awesome!

When vacation came, I was so excited. I tried snapping pictures out the car's window as we drove 55 miles per hour through the mountains. As we left Spokane, Washington, headed for Mount Rainier, it finally popped into view as we rounded a curve, and I snapped away – sure I would capture its beauty to the fullest. You can imagine my disappointment when I got my pictures developed after vacation. Mount Rainier looked like a blurred blob, smeared across the photo!

It didn't stop me, though. I received a Kodak Instamatic a few years later and learned to take better photos. In adulthood, my love of photography is still strong. Today, I have an insane obsession with photographing unique doors, beautifully rusted-out old cars, and macros of flowers and bugs! Photography taught me to appreciate the beauty in everything. I have no idea what happened to Fuzzy Waddles, and I wish I still had him and that old box camera.

Okay, let's go back to you as a child - the one who played pretend. Select two or three things you enjoyed or emersed yourself in as a child - such as painting or artwork, science projects, magic tricks, joke-telling, dancing, and so on. Has anything seeped its way into your adult life? Have you listened?

What does all this have to do with joy in your work? Oddly enough, everything.

What if your little self wasn't pretending, but really knew what direction to point you towards as an adult? What if...you listened?

You see, before pursuing my current job, I was a jewelry designer specializing in pearls (because #1), and I had to photograph all my jewelry which I LOVE doing (hence #3), and write the jewelry descriptions for each piece, too (cue #2).

Interesting, huh?

What do I do now?

I'm a copywriter and content marketing specialist writing mostly for jewelers and retailers. Although I'm known to write about serious stuff, too - using humor, of course (Thank you, Irma!), I sometimes get the urge to throw in a curse word or two because of my dad. Oh, and the photography – I do that simply for fun! I pretend I'm a photographer – and I love the hell out of it!

To find The Joy of Work, try taking what you love in life and pretending you can do anything and let go of restraints so you can do work that feeds your soul and enables you to find happiness along the way!

Shelly Buettner

Shelly Buettner is your Go-To Jewelry Copywriter and Content Marketing Specialist.

With a background and education in the jewelry industry, Shelly is a Certified Pearl Specialist with the Cultured Pearl Association of America (CPAA) and holds a diploma from the Gemological Institute of America (GIA) in the field of Pearls.

Shelly loves to blend her knowledge, education, and love for pearls and jewelry with her passion for writing and turn it into a fun and rewarding way to help people in their business.

With a mission to connect jewelry designers with their ideal clients through words, Ms. Buettner writes to empower jewelers to share their unique stories, amazing talents, and awe-inspiring creations with the jewelry lovers of the world.

Shelly offers her copywriting and content writing as well as proofreading and editing services to businesses in niches such as mind/body/spirit, mindset, and the luxury, travel, and real estate industries.

When not writing in her studio, she is often found scouring the internet for today's coolest jewelry trends, taking photos of beautiful old doors or rusted-out old cars, and snapping cool macro shots of flowers and bugs.

Connect with Shelly at www.shellybuettner.com.

CHAPTER 19

My Work Serves My Purpose

by Sheryl Lanette Mays

People describe work as a J.O.B., a place that pays the bills, puts food on our tables, and allows us to take a vacation. Plus, many other statements that show a lack of excitement and enjoyment for the thing we do daily. But there is another option. One that does allow you to be happy, to wake up every morning and be pleased to do the work that serves others. It's an affirmation that says *I am joyfully enjoying my work as it serves my purpose.*

I watched my father and mother work for more than 40 years at the same company. As most kids, I never asked if they were happy at work. For my entire childhood I never really knew what type of work they performed. During those times, the concept of *bring your child to work* wasn't a thing. I do remember being asked what my parents did and all I could muster up was they worked in a hospital. As I grew up, I learned that my father was an oncology technician and my mom was a surgery technician. I also remember my dad always taking additional classes obtaining certificates, certifications, and awards. But did they love their work?

I applaud my parents for their dedication to our family. Two very hard-working people climbing the ladder one step at a time. My dad died during my twenties. My mom at the age of retirement became an entrepreneur. Believe it or not, she purchased a nightclub. I don't think that would have ever happened had my dad remained alive. So, I watched the birth of an entrepreneur. A female in a male dominated field, a nightclub owner. And for the next 25 years she thrived in the entertainment industry. She also helped the community, sponsored teams, and left a legacy for our family. That work she loved! I watched her transform to a boss! And I loved it!

That was the beginning of my journey, seeds planted from my hard-working parents. My work that followed can be surmised with three life experiences. In the book *Power of Moments* by Chip and Dan Hearth, they share the concept of defining moments as being times in our lives that we list as unforgettable; those moments that bear a positive effect such as a basketball game victory, a promotion, a wedding, or obtaining a degree, the delightful moments that we share with others. According to the book, these moments are **EPIC** because they fulfill the requirements of **E**levation, **P**ride, **I**nsight, and **C**onnection. I believe when you have all four, you can truly experience the love of your work. But that doesn't always happen at the onset. That's what I learned from my parents; they learned to love the work by putting in the work.

My first job was at a fast food restaurant, where I learned about nepotism. I was hired by a cousin of my mom's best friend. Here I enjoyed the free milkshakes and fries on the regular. I also enjoyed that the manager was a family friend. I had my workdays selected according to my personal activity schedule. I could get off for school events, and I got a ride home. Sweet! Then my manager changed stores and left me with a different manager that wasn't so accommodating. My first taste of corporate change. So, I did what any non-committed employee would do … I quit!

But I learned a few lessons. Did I love the job? No. Were there moments of EPIC? I might have experienced such moments (in my connection to others and the insight of wanting more). The saying goes, "a job is what you do, when you are told what to do." Ouch. Because there was no thinking necessary, no creativity allowed, and no suggestions entertained.

Does this sound familiar? Are you in a no batteries required position? As a teenager, I had a few options. But what if you don't? What if you have to remain at a job that is neither fulfilling your passions, nor allowing you to experience growth? What can you do? Leave, but then how do you pay the bills and put food on the table? The correct answer is—you prepare for the exit. Yes, you write down the day you want to leave the company, that place that causes you to sit in the parking lot wondering if you should quit. I've been there. So write out your plan. What do you need to learn? Who do you need to meet? Then, take one step forward and ignite hope.

This has an effect on the brain that allows you to endure your time remaining because you know you have something in motion, something that will allow you to operate within your passion. You are creating your own defining moment. It might take time, but continue gathering, planting, and harvesting, then when you are *not* completely ready, take the chance. Move beyond your fears. If you wait until everything is perfectly aligned, the day may never come.

One of my favorite movies is "Hope Floats." During one of the scariest times in the daughter's life, her mom shared these words of wisdom. "Beginnings are scary, endings are sad, it's in the middle that counts because that's where hope floats."

My next memorable experience came many years later. I had a few jobs under my belt. The difference then was that I had life revelations. I found my gift, my voice, my strength, and my calling. Now I was in career mode. I had learned the difference between job and career. My vocabulary regarding my new vocation changed to more positive words. Picture it…it's the opening of The Drew Carey Show in the '90s. The doors of the store open up, employees run out into the streets dancing and singing. It was a defining moment for me … an insight. I WANTED A CAREER, a position where I could make a difference in the lives of others and benefit from the act of reciprocity ending the day feeling good about having touched someone in a remarkable way. It provided me with purpose.

Then it happened; I saw what seemed like a really cool career opportunity. I wasn't sure about the exact role, but I had spent the last 10 years speaking on behalf of several national nonprofit organizations. So, I gave it a shot and I applied for the position. I was hired as a high school coordinator for a career training institute. The duties were awesome. I got to travel my territory partnering with school districts, administration, clubs, and civic organizations. Now I was in a career. It was there that I took my first seat on a National Board of Directors. The high school coordinator role taught me how to build relationships, dissect data, create action plans, coach, create scripts and workshops, train, and communicate with senior leadership.

"The mind once stretched to a new idea, never return to its original dimensions."
Ralph Waldo Emerson

That statement has been proven true time and time again. Think about it. You're learning to navigate the corporate reins and you see more opportunities. You now realize the more you do, the more you can do. And then it happened. I was promoted to Regional Director. Now I led a team. Now I am a leader! But what kind of leader do I want to be? Here is where another lesson from my past job helped me gain insight into how I wanted to lead. My goal was to be an influential leader. I wanted to be a leader who would help others grow professionally by providing a healthy atmosphere where they felt empowered. This was my purpose. The reciprocity ... hearing others define the purpose of leadership, and how to keep employees engaged. The continued opportunity to learn from other leaders provided all the elements of EPIC. It was elevating, prideful, insightful and it bore connections. Then it happened again. I was promoted to Vice President of Admissions.

I brought all of what I learned, that mistakes I witnessed and even ones I had experienced. This was what I wanted. It was during that time that I traveled the country training, developing markets, hiring, partnering, mentoring, coaching, and developing company strategies. It was at that time that I realized what my father did. In the beginning of this chapter, I shared about my parents working at jobs never saying if they loved what they were doing. As I continued my corporate journey, I realized that my father *created* the love he had for his job. He came to love his job by continuing to learn and grow both personally and professionally. Eureka, that's it! That's how you learn to love your work. Until we find our true calling, we continue to gather skills, knowledge, cultivating relationships for future opportunities. We create our own defining moments.

"When you silence the chatter, you can move beyond your fears." I loved that role and remained there for 10 years. Then in 2014 the place where I was to retire ended. This opened another door and created another defining moment. It was through insight, connections, pride, and the feeling of elevation that I made the best decision in my life. I decided to silence the chatter, move beyond my fears, and walk into my impossibilities. Yes, I became an entrepreneur. Just like mom.

Today I work with clients assisting them in improving their customer experiences and customer care. I use everything I have learned and experienced for my clients' benefit. I also empower individuals to walk in their truth, be unapologetically bold, confidently moving beyond their fears, and walking into their impossibilities. I continue to operate within my purpose.

The life experiences I shared allow you to see that sometimes the job you have might not be the job for you, but what you learn from it can get you to the place you love. My father continued to learn more every opportunity he got, my mom took a chance and became a business owner.

What are you doing today? Are you disengaged, no longer a team player, becoming a clock watcher, using all of your sick time, wanting something more? Are you prepared for more? Are you taking steps for your exit? If you don't love your job today, and you still use the term job, then you need to prepare for your exit.

One of the most pervasive myths in the American culture is that we are entitled to a great life. Somehow, somewhere, someone, certainly not us, is responsible for filling our lives with continual happiness, exciting career options, nurturing family time and blissful relationships—because we exist. The real truth is that you're responsible for your life.

You must decide what you want. Ask yourself three questions.

How long would I like to do this?

Would I do this if I weren't getting paid?

Do I smile when I talk about what I do?

Loving your work changes your life when it's within your passion. It might not initially hit that sweet spot in your heart. It might start out with you saying, "it pays the bills, it puts food on the table, and it will do for now." Allowing that chatter to take residence in your mind you cease to operate within the power of positive thinking. That's the place where you take every experience, gleam insights, make connections, exude pride, and harness moments of elevation. You are deserving of a healthy work environment that allows you to grow and learn. You deserve a defining moment experience!

The place you find yourself in today has an opportunity to become a pathway leading to a defining moment, moments that allow you to be enthusiastic where you want to take on a new project. Only this time, instead of it being a daunting assignment, you look at it as an opportunity, one that allows you to learn new techniques, to partner with someone of influence, or be recognized for exceptional teamwork. This can provide credibility, increase your value, and allow you to rise and shine.

Look at it as a way to become visible. You now speak up at meetings, become part of the discussion and involved in the solutions. Leadership now asks for your opinion. When you are seen and heard, you stay on the minds of your leaders and when it comes time to make personnel changes, they look to you. You, the employee that went from unengaged to fully engaged.

- Get involved! Be willing to give a helping hand to make someone else shine. Showing that you can appreciate and value others is the quality of an influential leader.

- Be curious about how things get done. Ask to see what the connecting departments do regarding your work. Ask relevant questions on the strategic plan for the company. Show a genuine interest in the company's objective.

- Learn to be flexible because change is a constant. Be an early adapter of the new direction. Your role should be ever growing.

- And, finally, be supportive. There will always be different viewpoints, so be open to new ideas and give credit where due.

These are the life lessons I learned from my father about loving your work. Others might see it as a job, but you no longer use that term because you have purpose and a plan. Be careful as to the words you use to describe what you do, be positive. Remember, the journey begins in your mind. Life is unpredictable, but in everything you have a choice.

Sheryl Mays

Sheryl Mays is a Chief Experience Officer, 5x Author, International Speaker, On-Air Personality and Corporate Trainer. As the President of Rise and Shine Consulting and Coaching Firm, she provides consulting services and training for individuals, teams and organizations on customer experience, customer service and customer support. Sheryl is a contributing writer for Entrepreneur Magazine, Founder of Affirm Your Truth: The Affirmation Movement and Podcast Host, The Customers Tea.

Sheryl's latest endeavor is the one-of-a-kind online academy with a focus on customer service. Master the SALE Academy opened in July 2022.

Sheryl has a passion for creating experiences that will allow businesses to increase their referrals, sales and accelerate profits using a "breaking the script" concept leading to an increase in customer retention. She is an award-winning sales leader in the corporate world with more than 20 years of leadership experience.

A native of Buffalo, New York, with one daughter, a granddaughter and 2 furry friends, she holds a BS in Business Administration, Lean Six Sigma Black Belt, Neuro Linguistic Programming Practitioner, and a Jack Canfield Certified Trainer. She has held several positions volunteering with various civic organizations and is currently volunteering as an alumnus for Seminole State College, a counselor for SCORE Orlando, Seminole Chamber of Commerce, and actively involved with Women Entrepreneurs of America (WEA).

"I empower people to do the impossible, be unapologetically bold and confident."

Connect with Sheryl at www.risingandshine.com.

CHAPTER 20

Just LOVE

by Victoria Rader, Ph.D.

Work is love made visible. ~ Kahlil Gibran

"Once there was a little bunny...," my four-year-old son picked up the story, where my seven-year-old daughter left it off. Sleepy and semi-coherent, he went on to repeat the same made-up fairy tale she had just shared but substituting the main character with a *little bunny*. This was probably their fourth or fifth time through this tedious story creation I have challenged them to, as I was driving my tiny Fiat, completely lost on the island of Crete, with my two kids and mom.

With neither GPS nor cellular signal, we have travelled through Greek islands for three weeks, exploring, learning, and absorbing the richness of the culture. This was my first official homeschooling trip for my kids! I was living a dream...

Coming home, I realized that my dream has created a financial nightmare for my family! My husband patiently and lovingly, all things considered, explained to me that the piece of plastic I was swiping was not attached to a never-ending source of abundance. Turns out we did not have the money to cover our so-called educational expenses and I have officially welcomed my family into debt.

At that point, I not only knew theoretically but practical experience had shown me that, homeschooling and travelling were two great joys of my life. They were my **why**. I knew I needed to find a way to support it that did not involve either complete financial ruin or a divorce. I went to the computer and Googled, What is the fastest way to make money in the US while working from home? Yep, true story. The all-knowing Google suggested real estate. It was 2007, and I was learning the concept of a *hot market* and the millions of dollars promised to any blessed soul who would consider to be a realtor.

I pursued my real estate career with zeal and endurance and finally entered this promised land in, yes, 2008. Witnessing the beginning of a huge recession. Prices were falling. Agents were fleeing. I was clueless and overwhelmed. A perfect set up for success.

No really!

A perfect set up for success. I got HELP. I got a coach with Buffini and Coaching company adding another expense on my credit card. This was not an easy journey. Tough deals, difficult clients, moments of despair and anger at the banks, harming so many through misleading short sales, deep empathy for those that were losing their homes and those that could not qualify to even rent. I spent my first two years in real estate crying. Crying because I cared. Crying out of sheer exhaustion from serving my clients while schooling my kids. Crying from lack of sleep. Crying because it was cheaper than therapy. Just crying.

Amidst all the crying, a miracle was happening. The joy was dripping in. I was noticing how the pain, grief and disappointments were carving crevices in my soul that the joy started filling in. There was so much I disliked about the business. Except I loved my clients. I deeply loved my clients. In the end, love won.

When you learn to love what you do, God guides you to do what you love.

Within just the first few years of my real estate career, I became a top one percent of the agents in the US. I did this while homeschooling my kids, travelling the world and going to Disneyworld every year, while NOT working on Sunday. Yes, I was still crying a bit, but truly having so much more joy through SERVING my clients.

My success was noticed, I was invited to teach and do trainings for different real estate teams. The deeper joy filled my heart, the joy of teaching and training and coaching.

While conveying traditional success principles to others, I very quickly realized that what was most responsible for my success was not so much **what** I did. Although, yes, consistency is important, it was **how** I did what I did. I worked through LOVE.

To know how to better convey working through LOVE, I pursued my PhD in Metaphysical Sciences. I was coached by Bob Proctor and I mastered many modalities and techniques, stepping fully into my calling of being a coach, trainer, and speaker. LOVE became my acronym for **L**ife **O**riginating **V**ibrant **E**motion (Energy-in-Motion).

Then 2013 came to test my commitment to LOVE. They were the best of times and the worst of times. It was my best year in real estate and the year during which I lost eleven close family members and friends, all through different unexpected circumstances. Death came in to make an even deeper cavity in my soul. It came to define the meaning and the power of life. It came to remind me that only life mattered. Only life. Only Light. Only LOVE.

With each death my appreciation for life and my commitment to love grew. I surrendered to God's LOVE fully. Because I could not master strength of my own to make it from loss to loss to loss, I experienced joy through surrendering to God to carry me through. I still do. It is a daily beautiful challenge of joy to remember to let go and to let God.

So, following the still small voice of the Spirit, the comfortable knowing from God, I quit real estate, at the peak of my career, to open my YU2SHINE company.

Back to ground zero. Now with God as my full-time business partner! Yep, when you operate through LOVE as the fuel for your business, you get to lean into God as your business partner! After all, God is love. I had a calling to follow, and no clue how I was going to do it.

I had my daily clear guidance. It was always enough for me. Yet, as a leader with a few other partners, I had the capacity to convey the way, but not the how to. It was not only not enough for them, but it was also blinding and unfair. We were in misalignment and stagnation, and the original partnership fell apart.

I have re-organized and pursued my calling. I coached, did healing sessions, conducted seminars. I loved every moment of what I did. Because I was learning so much from the sessions and the seminars I was conducting, I felt I needed to start a YouTube channel.

After my first self-made gorgeous disaster of a video, my clients lovingly commented that the content was amazing, but they could barely hear me. No problem. I got a mic! Next video. Well, now they could hear me, but not really see me. No problem. I used a lamp on my daughter's piano. I have kept all of those videos on my channel, because now that I have hundreds of professional video podcasts with some of the top hosts in the world, I want to honor the joy of work without need for perfection.

So many of us rob ourselves of joy because we insist on being perfect. Only LOVE is perfect. When we do things through LOVE, we do them perfectly. Not because the results are perfect, but because the process is healing to us and to those that we are working with or performing for.

One of my dear clients and friends, having seen enough of my video explorations, had offered to become my videographer. A new fascinating stage of my business unfolded. More joy. More learning. More excitement.

Then someone watched one of my videos, over and over and over again until she took my seminar and in the same way that LOVE brought a videographer, the same LOVE brought her into my life as my marketing director. She, in turn, brought my web and app designer.

Client after client, student after student, my team started growing. Each finding a place guided by LOVE, with God as their primary partner and me as their secondary guide. LOVE continues to pour through every program, every book, every service and every app that we create. We create to fill the need, as guided by LOVE. This process, in turn, brings immense joy to each of us to the degree of which LOVE is present.

I often teach on the power of three minutes. Three minutes a day is enough to change a trajectory of your life. Knowing the power of meditation yet finding that very few of my clients were at a point in their life where they could devote long periods of time to meditating, we have created three-minute-long guided meditations to open infinite possibilities. We then included them in our Empower-mE app.

After all, **manifesting is transforming possibility into reality**. The process of converting this possibility is very tender, personal, and empowering.

1. Realize that there is a possibility. It is possible to be happy. It is possible to be financially free. It is possible to work through joy. *It is possible for someone.*

2. Give yourself a permission to partake of that possibility. *If it is possible for someone, what if it was possible for me?*

3. Affirm this possibility. *I know it is possible for me.*

4. Turn possibility into probability. *What action am I to take today to increase my probability of transforming this possibility into reality?*

Guiding others on the path of manifesting miracles as their reality brings me immense joy! In ManifestMiracles.mE free masterclass, I share how to create a life of infinite possibilities and miracles through understanding and harmonizing six mental faculties of the mindset: perception, imagination, intuition, reason, memory, and will.

1. **Perception:** Notice what you notice and how you notice it. Because what and how you notice what you do will create more of what you do. The fastest way out of a job you don't like is to find something you LOVE in it. Focus on that love, expand it. Find more things to love and focus on. As you continue to learn · to love what you do, your perception will expand to seek and find an opportunity to do what you love!

2. **Imagination:** Imagine a life in which you are full of joy while working. We cannot out-imagine our self-image. Our self-image

is a direct reflection of our own self-worth. A lot of us feel unworthy of a life we desire. To expand our imagination, we need to heal our connection to our infinite worth.

3. **Intuition:** With perception being the way we receive the world and imagination being the way we project back into it, intuition is that tuning fork that connects the two. When in tune with God, we hear our intuition clearly because we perceive the world as full of miracles and imagine ourselves to be an instrument of creation.

4. **Reason:** We can reason to support our intuition or to sabotage it. Daily, we are making a choice to either live because of someone else's limitations on us or to be the cause of our life. We reason either in favor of fear, of our scared little me or in favor of LOVE, of our Sacred mE (where **m** is a mortal matter that materially manifests, and **E** is Eternal Energy, the Essence that Expands).

5. **Memory:** We are to remember who we are as Eternal Energy so that we can surrender to LOVE by surrendering our mortal to Eternal, our matter to Energy, our material to Essential, and our manifesting to Expansive (more on that in my *Proser mE* book).

6. **Will:** Is our daily free will, free choice to choose either to surrender to God's will for us and through us, the divine guidance, the flow, the knowing, light, LOVE… or to resist divine will and to live a life of continued ego-struggle.

These six miraculous mindset faculties are inviting you to Perceive yourself as a miracle that you are, to Imagine a life full of joy, to follow your Intuition, to Reason through Memory of LOVE through following divine Will.

They invite you to just LOVE.

Victoria Rader, Ph.D.

Victoria Rader, Ph.D. is a Possibility Coach™, transformational speaker, founder of YU2SHINE, internationally best-selling author, creator of Empower-mE and Master-mE apps, founder of Free mE EFT and Quantum Freedom.

Victoria empowers her clients to grow in all areas of their life through the proven formula of success, so that they have more PEACE, PURPOSE, and PROSPERITY.

In 2009, during the recession, Victoria became a successful top one percent of real estate agents while homeschooling her kids. Victoria started training and seeing the limitations imposed by the subconscious mind. Later she received a PhD in Metaphysics to understand better how we create our daily reality. Victoria also got certified in many energy healing modalities and traditional success coaching approaches and has founded Free mE EFT and Quantum Freedom techniques as a way to free one's mind.

Victoria loves teaching on the universal/ God's laws and their practical daily application for people of faith and spiritual seekers, bridging the gap of judgement through LOVE (Life-Originating Vibrant Emotion).

She believes that you are a MIRACLE and that you are born to Manifest Miracles! (ManifestMiracles.mE).

Connect with Victoria at https://yu2shine.com.

READER BONUS!

Dear Reader,

As a thank you for your support, Action Takers Publishing would like to offer you a special reader bonus: a free download of our course, How to Write, Publish, Market & Monetize Your Book the Fast, Fun & Easy Way." This comprehensive course is designed to provide you with the tools and knowledge you need to bring your book to life and turn it into a successful venture.

The course typically **retails for $499**, but as a valued reader, you can access it for free. To claim your free download, simply follow this link ActionTakersPublishing.com/workshops - use the discount code "coursefree" to get a 100% discount and start writing your book today.

If we are still giving away this course by the time you're reading this book, head straight over to your computer and start the course now. It's absolutely free.

READER BONUS!

ActionTakersPublishing.com/workshops
discount code "coursefree"

Made in the USA
Las Vegas, NV
25 July 2023

75206829R00115